DYNAMIC SPIRITUAL
LEADERSHIP

Leading Like Paul

J. OSWALD SANDERS

DISCOVERY HOUSE
PUBLISHERS®

Feeding the Soul with the Word of God

Dynamic Spiritual Leadership: Leading Like Paul

Original edition, entitled *Paul the Leader,* © 1984 by J. Oswald Sanders
This edition © 1999 by Discovery House Publishers
All rights reserved.

Discovery House Publishers is affiliated with RBC Ministries, Grand Rapids, Michigan.

Discovery House books are distributed to the trade exclusively by Barbour Publishing, Inc., Uhrichsville, Ohio.

Requests for permission to quote from this book should be directed to: Permissions Department, Discovery House Publishers, P.O. Box 3566, Grand Rapids, MI 49501.

Library of Congress Cataloging-in-Publication Data
Sanders, J. Oswald
Dynamic Spiritual Leadership / J. Oswald Sanders.
    p. cm.
1. Consolation—Prayer-books and devotions—English. 2. Suffering—Religious aspects—Christianity. I. Title.
BV4909.L46   1993   248.8'6—dc20   92-31268

Interior design by Nick Richardson
Cover photo by Julie Richardson

ISBN: 978-1-57293-052-7

Printed in the United States of America

10 11 12 13 / / 9 8 7 6 5

Contents

About the Author

In the early 1920s, J. Oswald Sanders was a young lawyer busy at his practice in his native New Zealand. But God soon called him to a long career in teaching and administration at the Bible College of New Zealand in Auckland, and later to an even longer career with the China Inland Mission (now the Overseas Missionary Fellowship). He was the mission's general director during the decades of great change following World War II, when the mission's personnel were forced out of China but established new works throughout the rest of East Asia.

Upon his retirement as OMF general director in 1969, he served as principal of the Christian Leaders Training College in Papua New Guinea.

Throughout the years, Dr. Sanders wrote many books. He also spent his time engaged in a worldwide teaching ministry until he lost his brief battle with cancer. Dr. Sanders died in 1992 in New Zealand. He was ninety years old.

PREFACE

This volume is the outcome of a request that I follow up my book *Spiritual Leadership* with another enunciating the leadership principles from the life and ministry of the apostle Paul. I realize that many more important works on Paul have come from more able pens, but I have not yet found one that specifically treats Paul's life from this angle.

In the preparation of this material I acknowledge special indebtedness to a small volume published at the beginning of the century (1910): *The Man Paul* by Robert E. Speer, Secretary of the American Presbyterian Board of Foreign Missions. It is an extremely perceptive and valuable study of the apostle. I have followed his example in including some appropriate verses from F. W. H. Myers' magnificent poem, "Saint Paul."

It is my hope that this book may prove helpful in individual Bible study and in home groups. With this in view, I have included copious Scripture references.

1

A MAN JUST LIKE US

"We . . . are only men, human like you."

ACTS 14:15

The strong, sure, and charismatic leadership so desperately needed in our confused age seems to be conspicuously lacking. One concerned citizen, disturbed by prevailing conditions and the inability of his nation's leaders to find a panacea for their ills, made this comment: "The critical juncture found none but second-rate actors on the political stage, and the decisive moment was neglected because the courageous were deficient in power, and the powerful in sagacity, courage and resolution."[1]

That sounds strangely contemporary, yet it was written a century ago by one Friedrich Stiller. Have things changed essentially in the intervening years? Our Lord's graphic words are proving true, accurately diagnosing conditions today: "On the earth, nations will be in anguish and perplexity at the roaring and tossing of the sea" (Luke 21:25).

World conditions have worsened immeasurably since the

time this statement was made, but the same appraisal of the situation would be appropriate. Each generation has to meet and resolve it own leadership problems, and today we are facing an acute crisis in leadership in many spheres. Crisis succeeds crisis, yet our leaders come up with few solutions, and the prognosis is by no means reassuring.

The church has not escaped this dearth of authoritative leadership. Her voice, which once sounded a clarion call of hope to beleaguered humanity, is now strangely muted, and her influence in the world community has become minimal. The salt has largely lost its savor, and the light its radiance.

Merely to bemoan this state of affairs is counter-productive. A more constructive approach would be to discover afresh the principles and factors that inspired the dynamic spiritual leadership of Paul and the other apostles in the golden days of the church. We need not only to discover them, but to endeavor to apply them to our own situation. Spiritual principles are timeless; they do not change from generation to generation.

"WARTS AND ALL"

A friend once remarked to me, "Isn't it a humbling thing to see one's own faults running around on two little legs?" When we see them embodied in someone else, our faults become painfully obvious to us. Similarly, we more readily grasp spiritual principles when we see them embodied in personality than when formulated as mere academic propositions.

This is why one of the most rewarding Bible studies is to trace in the lives of men and women just like us the interplay of divine providence and human personality—to discover how the conditions and experiences of early life were controlled and shaped by a skillful and beneficent Hand.

We must be grateful that divine inspiration has ensured the preservation and selection of the providential factors involved. The plain, unvarnished facts are recorded in a straightforward manner, and with no attempt to retouch the photograph. The Bible is careful to portray its characters as they really were, "warts and all."

It is in our Lord and not in Paul that we see the ideal of leadership, for he is a Leader *par excellence.* There are some, however, who find Jesus Christ's very perfection daunting and rather discouraging. Because he inherited no sinful nature as we do, they feel that this fact conferred on him a vast advantage, and removed him from the arena of their earthly struggles and failures. He seems so far above them that they are able to draw very little practical help from his shining example. While this viewpoint springs from a misconception of the nature of the help Christ is able to extend, its results are very real.

In the apostle Paul God has provided the example of *"a man just like us"* (James 5:17). True, he was a man of towering spiritual stature, but he was also a man who knew failure along with his success. Even as he cried out in his despair, "What a wretched man I am! Who will rescue me from this body of death?" he exulted, "Thanks be to God—through Jesus Christ our Lord!" (Romans 7:24-25).

These and similar outpourings of his heart bring him into our street, where we can more easily indentify with his experiences. He was not "an impossible, lofty saint," but a frail, fallible man just like us—someone who can speak to our need.

Thus in Christ we find inspiration from a real Man who

never failed, while in Paul we gain encouragement from a man who fell and rose again. "A perfect man reveals what the ideal is; a man defeated and finally victorious discloses what by the grace of God we may become . . . . We need Jesus on one side of us and Paul on the other if we are to walk in triumph along the difficult and perilous way.[2]

If our study of Paul's leadership principles is to be permanently fruitful, it must be more than academic. Each person, in his own life and sphere of service, will need to master and translate them into action. The facts must become factors of experience.

We should be grateful to Paul for the unconscious self-revelation that characterizes his letters. We learn far more about him from his own indirect and unstudied references in his letters than we do from Luke's historical material in the book of Acts. In his biography of the late A. W. Tozer, D. J. Fant adopted the method of interpreting the man from his own writings, and this is the method that will be followed in these studies.

In Paul we find an inspiring prototype of what one man, wholly abandoned to God, can achieve in a single generation. Thus it will be our purpose to view him especially in his role as a leader in the church—to consider his viewpoint on relevant subjects, to examine the qualities that made him the man he was, and to discover how these traits contributed to his superb leadership.

Notes

1. *Newsweek,* April 21, 1980, 4.

2. Jefferson, Charles E., *The Character of Paul* (New York: Macmillan, 1924), 32.

2
THE PREPARATION
OF A PIONEER

*We were under great pressure, far beyond our ability to endure,
so that we despaired even to life. Indeed, in our hearts we felt the
sentence of death. But this happened that we might not rely
on ourselves but on God, who raises the dead.*

2 CORINTHIANS 1:8-9

From his earliest days of which we have a record, Paul displayed incipient qualities of leadership which developed with the years. Although we must avoid the error of attributing to him almost superhuman qualities and sanctity, we cannot escape the conclusion that he was a man of impressive stature and personality—one of those colossal figures who impress themselves indelibly on history. And yet a closer study reveals a vulnerable, lovable "man of like passions," whose life was rendered extraordinary by a more than ordinary faith and an unreserved surrender to his Master.

He has been nominated the world's most successful Christian, and his career has been considered the most astonishing in world history. Perhaps no other has attained the same heights in so many capacities. His versatility was such that in retrospect it seems as though he possessed almost every gift. But despite Paul's awe-inspiring record, in his writings he successfully establishes rapport with the humble believer as easily as with the erudite philosopher.

A present-day parallel to the apostle, it has been suggested, would be a man who could speak Chinese in Peking, quoting Confucius and Mencius, could write closely reasoned theology in English and expound it at Oxford, and could defend his cause in Russian before the Soviet Academy of Sciences.

In his book, *The Man Who Shook the World,* John Pollock tells of the impression a study of Paul's life and work made on him: "A biographer's nose develops a sort of instinct, and it was not long before I was struck by the credibility, the genuineness of the person who was emerging from the Acts of the Apostles and the Epistles taken as a whole. A convincing character with a completely credible if astonishingly unusual story."[1]

In autobiographical references in his letters, Paul pictures himself before his conversion as a moral, successful, and law-abiding citizen. At that time he saw little reason for self-reproach, and evidenced no sense of being under the disfavor of God. Indeed, if anything, he felt the reverse. He had been no prodigal. He could place his life alongside the law of God without any undue sense of having failed to meet its obligations.

But his excessive zeal found unworthy expression in his ruthless persecution of the followers of the Christ. These qualities combined to make him one of the most difficult persons to convert to Christianity, for he was so entirely convinced of his own integrity.

His complex personality was unified, however, by a remarkable singleness of purpose. His immense intellectual powers alone would have made him someone to be remembered, even if he had never become a Christian. Of all the apostles, he alone was an intellectual, and this fact was to prove of great significance in the progress of the new faith. For Christianity to make an intellectual as well as a moral and spiritual conquest of the world, it needed someone of Paul's mental caliber to explain and enforce the significance of Christ's death and resurrection, and other related doctrines.

Most of the other apostles displayed some distinctive gift or trait of character, but Paul's character was so many-sided that in him they all seemed to coalesce. Peter, for example, was an extremist, and Andrew a conservative. In Paul both qualities are evident. On occasion he was as venturesome and impetuous as Peter, but if necessary he could be as cautious as Andrew. He was conservative where principle was involved, but equally prepared to adopt radical methods to attain his end.

Where principle was clearly at stake Paul was inflexible and would not yield for a moment, even if the person involved was the prestigious apostle Peter. Because the vastly important issue of Christian liberty was at issue, Paul told the Galatians, "We did not give in to them for a moment, so that the truth of the gospel might remain with you" (Galatians 2:5). But when only a preference and not a principle was involved, he was prepared to make large concessions.

HEREDITY AND EARLY TRAINING

Heredity bears an important part in any life. In the providence of God, the preparation of a leader begins before birth. Jeremiah recognized this sovereign activity of God when he recorded the Lord's word to him: "Before I formed you in the womb I knew you, before you were born I set you apart; I appointed you as a prophet to the nations" (Jeremiah 1:5). He was predestined to leadership, but he was to discover that his preparation would involve a long and sometimes painful training course. Paul was also conscious that he was the subject of a determining and beneficent will, although the path ahead unfolded only slowly before him.

> What to thee is shadow, to Him is day,
>   And the end He knoweth;
> And not on a blind and aimless way,
>   The spirit goeth.
> Like warp and woof, all destinies
>   Are woven fast,
> Linked in sympathy, like the keys
>   Of an organ vast.
>
> —*J. G. Whittier*

It would have been around A.D. 33 when Paul stood guard over the clothes of the men who stoned Stephen. He was then described as "a young man" (Acts 7:58), a term that could be applied to an age range extending from twenty to over thirty years old. If, as seems most likely, he was then a member of the prestigious Sanhedrin, he must have been over thirty, the qualifying age for that judicial body. This would mean that he was born about the same time as Jesus. In a sermon attributed to John Chrysostom, it is inferred that he was born in the year 2 B.C. On the supposition that he died about A.D. 66, he would have been about sixty-eight years old when he was executed.

As to heredity, Paul came from a moderately affluent family, for they met the property qualification required for citizens of Tarsus. His parents, who were of the tribe of Benjamin, named their son after his illustrious tribal ancestor, King Saul. Since his father was a Roman citizen, they added the Latin name, Paulus. This Roman citizenship placed him among the aristocracy of Tarsus.

Since Paul's father was a strict Pharisee, he no doubt fulfilled for his son all the ceremonial requirements of the Judaic law with meticulous care. Paul himself said that he had been trained scrupulously in the best traditions of the Pharisees. Tragically enough, this formerly Puritan-like body of the Sanhedrin had by Paul's day become infected with legalism and hypocrisy.

Paul was obviously proud of his pedigree and attainments of which he wrote to the Philippian believers, "If anyone else thinks he has reasons to put confidence in the flesh, I have more: circumcised on the eighth day, of the people of Israel, of the tribe of Benjamin, a Hebrew of Hebrews; in regard to the law, a Pharisee; as for zeal, persecuting the church; as for legalistic righteousness, faultless" (Philippians 3:4-6). "Under Gamaliel I was thoroughly trained in the law of our fathers" (Acts 22:3). Thus all the formative years were calculated to prepare him to be an eminent Pharisee and rabbi, like his great mentor Gamaliel.

Paul's family spoke Greek and he was also familiar with Aramaic (Acts 22:2). From his earliest years, he was familiar with the Greek Septuagint version of the Old Testament, large portions of which he committed to memory.

His early education was either at home or in a school connected with the synagogue, for his scrupulous parents would have been unlikely to entrust him to Gentile teachers.

Like all boys of good families, he learned a trade. St. Francis Xavier worked with his hands, and expressed the wish that all Christian brothers would do the same. Gamaliel held that learning of any kind unaccompanied by a trade ended in nothing but sin.

Paul's trade of tentmaking proved a valuable asset in the years ahead. His native Tarsus abounded with mountain goats, whose long hair was woven into strong outer garments or into tents made from material known as Cilician cloth. The value of this trade to Paul was that it could be pursued anywhere and required no costly equipment.

He was proud of his native city of Tarsus, describing it as "no ordinary city" (Acts 21:39). It was one of the three great university cities of the Roman Empire, the others being Athens and Alexandria, and was said to surpass its rivals in intellectual eminence. Its scholarly atmosphere had doubtless already influenced the youth's eager mind.

At the age of about fifteen, he took the journey to Jerusalem, where he may have lived with his sister (Acts 23:16). It is interesting to observe that apparently some of his relatives had embraced Christianity before he did (Romans 16:7). In Jerusalem he would have seen and heard the exciting sights and sounds of the temple service, watching with reverence the officiating priests and the ascending smoke from the sacrificial altar.

One of the many clear evidences of divine providence shaping Paul's life was the fact that, probably through the influence of his family, he was privileged to sit at the feet of Gamaliel, who was called "the beauty of the Law." This learned and notable rabbi was one of seven Jewish doctors of the law to whom was given the honored title of "Rabban." He was of the school of Hillel, which embraced a broader and more liberal view than that of Shammai.

Paul was thus exposed to a wider spectrum of teaching than would otherwise have been the case. Unlike Shammai, Gamaliel was interested in Greek literature and encouraged Jews to have friendship and social intercourse with foreigners. From him young Saul probably learned sincerity and honesty of judgment, as well as a willingness to study and use the works of Gentile authors.

It was this same Gamaliel who counseled moderation when the crowd would have killed Peter and the other apostles. "A pharisee named Gamaliel, a teacher of the law, who was honored by all the people, stood up in the Sanhedrin and. . . . addressed them: . . . . 'In the present case I advise you: Leave these men alone! Let them go! For if their purpose or activity is of human origin, it will fail. But if it is from God, you will not be able to stop these men; you will only find yourselves fighting against God'" (Acts 5:34-39).

After his training under Gamaliel, as a qualified and recognized Pharisee Paul returned home until he was old enough to embark on his life task.

In passing it may be noted that since Gamaliel did not give

sanction to persecuting activities, it is difficult to account for the subsequent unbridled fury of his pupil, unless it was the outward expression of a fierce battle that raged within his breast. "He was as much at war with himself as he was with the Christians."[2]

Academically, Paul made spectacular progress. He surpassed his fellow students in both academic achievement and zeal. He was "zealous for God" (Acts 22:3), and "extremely zealous for the traditions of my fathers" (Galatians 1:14). It is not difficult to imagine the fury of the Jewish authorities at the loss of his promising leadership.

As already mentioned, Paul was almost certainly at one time a member of the Sanhedrin, the supreme Jewish legal and civil court. To have been eligible for this honor, he would have been over thirty years old at the time of Stephen's death. Paul himself says he was one of the judges who voted in favor of the death of the Christians. "On the authority of the chief priests I put many of the saints in prison, and when they were put to death, I cast my vote against them." (Acts 26:10).

In those days it was customary to marry at an early age, and for one to hold a seat on the Sanhedrin, he had to be a married man. The reason behind this provision was that members were supposed to lean toward mercy, and a husband and father would be more likely to possess that quality than an unmarried man. The weight of evidence would thus seem to be in favor of Paul having been a married man, but Scripture is silent on the subject. There is a tradition that he was a widower. It may have been that after his conversion to Christianity he was disowned and repudiated by his family.

Personal Advantages

The overruling hand of God in training Paul for leadership may be clearly discerned in the advantages he enjoyed as a result of both his heredity and his environment.

And what was true in Paul's case is as true for us all. A providence is shaping our ends; a plan is developing in our lives; a supremely wise and loving Being is making all things work together for good. In the sequel of our life's story we shall see that there was a meaning and necessity in all the previous incidents, save those which are the result of our own folly and sin, and that even those have been made to contribute to the final result.[3]

It is doubtful that there was any other Christian man of the first century who united in himself most of the qualities and qualifications that would constitute him a world citizen—a Jew with Roman citizenship living in a Greek city. Both by birth and training Paul possessed the tenacity of the Jew, the practicality of the Roman, and the culture of the Greek; these qualities enabled him to adapt to the polyglot peoples among whom he was to move.

These qualities also uniquely fitted Paul to be a world missionary leader. To a Roman citizen there was no such thing as a foreign land, so the vexed question of extra-territoriality that has plagued missionary work for so long was no problem for him. Visas and passports had not yet been thought of. Paul could never travel beyond his own flag, and since a similar type of civilization existed throughout the Roman Empire, there were few cultural barriers to surmount. Also there were few major social, economic, or currency problems to be overcome. His Roman citizenship proved a great boon to him on several occasions. And since Greek was almost universally known, language problems were minimal.

Because he had gained his theological education at the feet of Jewry's most famous rabbi, no one could justly impugn Paul's scholarship or extensive knowledge of the Law. Then, too, he was equally familiar with the philosophical system of his day and could dispute with their proponents on their own ground. "He spoke and argued with the Hellenists" (Acts 9:29 NRSV).

His tentmaking skill relieved him of the disadvantage of being a financial burden on the emerging churches, and the pressures that financial obligations often generate were thus obviated. This afforded him a freedom to counsel or rebuke people in the church, which would have been much more difficult had he been financially obligated to them.

PERSONAL HANDICAPS

Many missionary leaders today would gladly welcome many of the advantages Paul enjoyed. But these advantages were probably more than counterbalanced by the severe handicaps under which he and his colleagues had to work.

In *The Old Tea House*, Violet Alleyn Storey writes: "'Let those who think they are handicapped by some affliction in body or in spirit for a noble work in life remember Paul,' one has said. Milton the blind who looked on Paradise! Beethoven the deaf who heard vast harmonies! Byron the lame who climbed towards Alpine skies! Who pleads a handicap, remember these."

Often Paul had no suitable place in which to preach. Before long he was regarded as a dangerous troublemaker, and the synagogues were closed to him.

In order to support himself, and sometimes others too, at times he had to toil night and day. The wonder is that he still found time for effective gospel witness.

He apparently suffered the handicap of being far from impressive physically. "Some say," he wrote, "'His letters are weighty and forceful, but in person he is unimpressive'" (2 Corinthians 10:10).

In *The Acts of Paul and Hecla,* a novel written in the second or third century, there is the only pen portrait of Paul still in existence. In it the apostle is described as "small in size with meeting eyebrows, with a rather large nose, bald-headed, bow-legged, strongly built, full of grace, for at times he looked like a man and at times he had the face of an angel."[4]

Though not cast in a herculean mold, he displayed incredible physical stamina, for throughout his ministry bodily suffering and discomfort were routine.

Paul was apparently not considered by some to be an impressive orator, as was Apollos. "His letters are weighty . . . but . . . his speaking amounts to nothing" (2 Corinthians 10:10).

False teachers and legalists dogged his steps and endeavored to neutralize and dissipate his work. They impugned his apostleship and belittled his authority, compelling him to reluctantly defend himself and vindicate his divine appointment.

Paul suffered the acute pain arising from disaffection among his beloved colleagues—Barnabas, Demas, Hymenaeus, and Philetus, to name a few. Such breaches of fellowship were desperately painful to his warm and generous pastor's heart. To fill his cup of bitterness, he wrote on one occasion, "Everyone in the province of Asia has deserted me, including Phygelus and Hermogenes" (2 Timothy 1:15). This was a shattering blow to the hard-pressed leader. Then, too, some of his converts were not steadfast, becoming a weight on his heart.

Burdens of the heart and acute physical sufferings and hardships were routine for Paul: weariness and pain, hunger and thirst, cold and nakedness, scourging and imprisonment, stoning and shipwreck, perils on both land and sea were part and parcel of his missionary experience (2 Corinthians 11:23-28). He summed it up in one sentence: "[Our bodies] had no rest, but we were harassed at every turn—conflicts on the outside, fears within" (2 Corinthians 7:5).

This dedicated apostle worked under constant pressure, yet without being submerged by it. "We were under great pressure, far beyond our ability to endure, so that we despaired even of life" (2 Corinthians 1:8). But the pressure in the life of Paul was usually productive: "This happened that we might not rely on ourselves but on God" (1:9). In addition to all the other incidental pressures was the overarching burden of responsibility for the well-being of the churches he had helped to bring into existence. "Besides everything else, I face daily the pressure of my concern for all the churches" (2 Corinthians 11:28).

Such an intolerable load would have crushed a lesser man. But Paul was a man who had mastered the secret of casting his burden on the Lord on the one hand, and appropriating his abundantly sufficient grace on the other.

The apostle's attitude toward these handicaps was exemplary, and is instructive to all who are in positions of leadership.

He did not passively and reluctantly endure them; he reached the high ground of actually glorying in them and in the opportunity they afforded of proving and displaying the sufficiency of Christ and the adequacy of his grace.

Paul had traveled a great distance along the road to spiritual maturity when he was able to say, "For Christ's sake, I delight in weaknesses, in insults, in hardships, in persecutions, in difficulties. For when I am weak, then I am strong" (2 Corinthians 12:10). He did not consider these trials to be unmitigated evils, but he valued them as instruments designed to conform him to the image of Christ. Paradoxically, the trials became channels of grace, and occasions for rejoicing.

THE CONVERSION OF A RELIGIOUS MAN

The crucial importance of Paul's conversion in the history of the church is attested to by the fact that the Holy Spirit caused three full-length, complementary accounts of that event to be preserved in the Scriptures. In light of his subsequent and continuing influence, it is not too much to say that his conversion was one of the epochal events of history. Only one other such event is reported in fuller detail: the crucifixion of the Son of God.

Paul had actively participated in the infamous stoning of Stephen. "When the blood of your martyr Stephen was shed," he confessed, "I stood there giving my approval and guarding the clothes of those who were killing him" (Acts 22:20). It may have been this evidence of his persecuting zeal that led to his election to the Sanhedrin, and later to his appointment as an inquisitor against Christianity.

According to his own account, he embarked on his grisly task with fanatical intensity. "I persecuted the followers of the Way to their death, arresting both men and women and throwing them into prison, as also the high priest and all the Council can testify. I even obtained letters from them to their brothers in Damascus, and went there to bring these people as prisoners to Jerusalem to be punished" (Acts 22:4-5). He went even further in his malignant zeal: "I tried to force them to blaspheme. In my obsession against them, I even went to foreign cities to persecute them" (Acts 26:11).

It was while traveling the Damascus road on a persecuting foray that the young rabbi was suddenly stopped in his tracks. In vivid words Paul recounted to King Agrippa that shattering and unforgettable experience that turned the persecutor into the preacher: "About noon, O king, as I was on the road, I saw a light from heaven, brighter than the sun, blazing around me and my companions. We all fell to the ground, and I heard a voice saying to me in Aramaic, 'Saul, Saul, why do you persecute me? It is hard for you to kick against the goads'" (Acts 26:13-14).

Now without doubt Saul had been deeply affected by Stephen's demeanor in his martyrdom. Sir William Ramsay's suggestion is that Paul was so sure that the impostor Jesus was dead that when Stephen's vision was repeated in his own experience, the whole ground of his hostility collapsed.

Evidently the most astounding thing to Paul was that when Christ appeared to him it was not in wrath and vengeance, but in boundless, unconditional love. It was this factor that shattered his last opposition and melted the hardness of his intransigent heart.

All merciful, almighty Lord,
We bless the love—its depth and height,
Which made by Thy transforming Word
Thy foe a burning shining light,
A chosen messenger of God,
    Eternity o'ershading time,
Whose bleeding feet unwearied trod
    From shore to shore, from clime to clime.
                              —*E. H. Bickersteth*

One of the most exhaustive studies of this epochal event was made in the eighteenth century by Lord Lyttelton, a parliamentarian whose name appeared in every major political debate in the British Parliament, and who held the office of Chancellor of the Exchequer in the Cabinet. He was a man of letters as well as a politician.

In his treatise embodying the results of his investigation, Lyttelton recounts that he and his lawyer friend Gilbert West were both convinced that the Bible was an imposture, and they determined to expose the fraud. Lyttelton chose the conversion of Paul, and West chose the resurrection of Christ, the two most crucial points of Christianity, as the subjects of their hostile research.[5]

Each approached his study sincerely, though full of prejudice, but the result of their separate research, which extended over a considerable period, was that both were converted to faith in Christ through their very efforts to discredit the biblical record. When at last they came together, it was not to exult over the exposé of another imposture but to felicitate each other on their discovery that the Bible was indeed the Word of God.

In the opening paragraph of his treatise, Lyttelton wrote: "The conversion and apostleship of Paul alone, duly considered was of itself a demonstration sufficient to prove Christianity to be a divine revelation." So convincing was Lyttelton's work that the famous Samuel Johnson declared it to be a treatise "to which infidelity has never been able to fabricate a specious answer."

Lyttelton laid down four propositions which in his consideration exhausted all the possibilities of the case concerning Paul's conversion: (1) Paul was an impostor who said what he knew to be false; (2) he was an enthusiast who imposed ideas on himself by the force of an overheated imagination; (3) he was deceived by the fraud of others; or (4) what he declared to be the cause of his conversion really did happen, and therefore the Christian religion is a divine revelation.

Lyttelton went on to demonstrate from Scripture that Paul was not an impostor. What motive, he asked, could have induced him, while journeying to Damascus with a heart filled with insensate hatred against the sect, to completely turn around, becoming a disciple of Christ? Motive was absent. Paul had betrayed no desire for wealth or reputation from his association with the group. Nor was he seeking power, for his whole life was marked by a complete absence of self-seeking. Nor was he motivated by a desire for the gratification of any other passion, for his writings urge the strictest morality.

On the other hand, to become a Christian was to incur hatred and contempt, as well as to expose himself to danger. Would he have endured the "loss of all things," and exulted in what he knew to be a fraud? That would be an imposture as unprofitable as it was perilous. So Lyttelton's conclusion was that this theory defeated itself.

One interesting sidelight is that Paul appealed to King Agrippa's personal knowledge of the truth of his conversion story. Paul stated, "What I am saying is true and reasonable. The king is familiar with these things, and I can speak freely to him. I am convinced that none of this has escaped his notice, because it was not done in a corner" (Acts 26:25-26).

In itself this is a remarkable proof of both the public knowledge of the facts and the integrity of the man who could fearlessly call on the king to give testimony for him. If the story of Paul's conversion had been fabricated for the occasion, why would the godly Ananias have gone to meet such a monster there in Damascus (Acts 9:10-19)?

From these and other arguments, Lyttelton drew two final conclusions: (1) Paul was not a cheat, telling a trumped-up tale about his conversion; (2) if he were, he could not have succeeded.

Although it had been preceded by a long period of unconscious "incubation," Paul's was undoubtedly a sudden conversion. He had been unable to banish from his mind the face of the dying martyr—"like the face of an angel" (Acts 6:15).

> He heeded not reviling tones
> Nor sold his heart to idle moans,
> Though cursed and scorned and bruised with stones.
> But looking upward, full of grace,
> He prayed, and from a happy place
> God's glory smote him on the face.
>
> —*Lord Tennyson*

Nor could he forget Stephen's last poignant prayer: "Lord, do not hold this sin against them" (Acts 7:60).

The ever active Holy Spirit had set the stage over the years for this grand confrontation and capitulation. The blinding flash found a vast amount of inflammable material in the heart of the young persecutor.

The miracle occurred in the full blaze of the noonday sun. Paul looked upon Jesus in all His Messianic glory and majesty. We know that this was no mere subjective vision, for Paul ranks it as the last *appearance* of the Savior and places it on the same level as his appearances to the other apostles and disciples. His statement is clear and unequivocal: "He appeared to Peter, and then to the Twelve. After that, he appeared to more than five hundred of the brothers at the same time, most of whom are still living, though some have fallen asleep. Then he appeared to James, then to all the apostles, and last of all *he appeared to me also,* as to one abnormally born" (1 Corinthians 15:5-8).

It was not an ecstasy, but a real and objective appearance of the risen and exalted Christ, clothed in his glorified humanity. Paul was immediately convinced that He was no impostor.

The whole event has been epitomized in verse by Amos R. Wells:

> The light was brighter than the noonday sun, the flaming glory of
> the Holy One.
> It showed the crucified, the Nazarene, splendid in majesty,
> benign, serene,
> Blinding with Deity's effulgent blaze, the font of power and the
> home of praise.

It showed, in cowering shame before them all, the cruel,
    persecuting heart of Saul

His bigotry, his madness, and his pride, and Stephen's martyr
    glory as he died.

So piercing was the overpowering light, it blasted utterly all other
    sight,

It whelmed in blackness all the world abroad, and centered vision
    on the Son of God.

Roused by that light, Saul's conscience woke at last, shrank from
    the horrid turmoil of the past,

And saw how all his life, by passion marred, had kicked against
    the pricks and found it hard.

The light flamed full on duty, sent a ray forth to the future's hope
    of brightening day.

"What shall I do, Lord?" Hear the trembling call born of a new
    regenerated Saul.

And then, dear sight restored, the light divine continued grandly
    governing to shine.

It sent the apostle nobly forth again, Christ's witness to the world
    of groping men,

Till all the lands of misery and night glowed in the dawning of
    the heavenly light.[6]

What a different entrance into Damascus it was from what
the inquisitor had envisaged! "He fell to the ground and heard
a voice say to him '. . . Now get up and go into the city, and
you will be told what you must do.' . . . Saul got up from the
ground, but when he opened his eyes he could see nothing.
So they led him by the hand into Damascus" (Acts 9:4-8). A
captive chained to the chariot wheel of his embarking on an

unknown but auspicious course. All was dark without, but all was light within.

Paul's surrender to the lordship of Christ was immediate and absolute. The moment he realized that Jesus was no impostor but the Messiah of the Jews, he knew there could be only one appropriate response. The whole story is epitomized in his two questions: "Who are you, Lord?" and "What shall I do, Lord?" (Acts 22:8, 10). True conversion always results in seeking and then yielding to the will of God, for all saving faith involves obedience (Romans 1:5).

> The proudest heart that ever beat
> Hath been subdued in me;
> The wildest will that ever rose
> To scorn Thy cause or aid Thy foes
> Is quelled, my God, by Thee.
> —W. Hone

How amazing was the victorious strategy of God in the life of Paul of Tarsus!

The bitterest foe became the greatest friend. The blasphemer became the preacher of Christ's love. The hand that wrote the indictment of the disciples of Christ when he brought them before magistrates and into prison now penned epistles of God's redeeming love. The heart that once beat with joy when Stephen sank beneath the bloody stones now rejoiced in scourgings and stonings for the sake of Christ. From this erstwhile enemy, persecutor, blasphemer came the greater part of the New Testament, the noblest statements of theology, the sweetest lyrics of Christian love.[7]

—*C. E. Macartney*

THE CALL TO SERVE

The call of God came to Paul in so clear and specific a manner that he could not mistake it. While the apostle was in Damascus, blinded by the heavenly light, Ananias came to him to communicate the message he had received from God. Just as Paul was regaining his sight, Ananias said, "The God of our fathers has chosen you to know his will and to see the Righteous One and to hear the words from his mouth. You will be his witness to all men of what you have seen and heard" (Acts 22:14-15).

Later, when he returned to Jerusalem, Paul "fell into a trance and saw the Lord speaking. . . . Then the Lord said to [Paul] . . . . 'Go; I will send you far away to the Gentiles'" (Acts 22:17-18, 21). To the understandably fearful Ananias, who was commissioned by God to welcome the notorious persecutor into the Christian church, God also indicated the sphere of witness to which he had called Paul. "The Lord said to Ananias, 'Go! This man is my chosen instrument to carry my name before the Gentiles and their kings and before the people of Israel. I will show him how much he must suffer for my name'" (Acts 9:15-16).

Paul revealed another facet of his call when he defended himself before Agrippa. "I heard a voice saying to me . . . 'Get up and stand on your feet. I have appeared to you to appoint you as a servant and as a witness of what you have seen of me and what I will show you. I will rescue you from your own people and from the Gentiles. I am sending you to them to open their eyes and turn them from darkness to light, and from the power of Satan to God'" (Acts 26:14-18).

Thus from the earliest days of his Christian life, he not only knew that he was a chosen medium through whom God would communicate His revelation, but he had a general idea of what God had planned for his future. He knew that (1) his ministry would take him far from his home, (2) he would have a special ministry to the Gentiles, and (3) this ministry would involve him in great suffering. Only gradually did he come to realize that this call was not so much a new purpose of God for his life as it was the culmination of the preparatory process that began before his birth.

It is the same today. The call of the missionary is not so much a new purpose for his life as it is the discovery of the purpose for which God brought him into the world. The Lord said to His disciples that positions of leadership in His kingdom were according to the sovereign appointment of His Father. "These places belong to those for whom they have been prepared" (Mark 10:40). Paul recognized this, but he came only gradually into clear understanding of what God's work was for him.

It was only after the Jews had consistently rejected his message that Paul devoted himself almost exclusively to the Gentiles. His experience in Corinth brought things to a head. "Paul devoted himself exclusively to preaching, testifying to the Jews that Jesus was the Christ. But when the Jews opposed Paul and became abusive, he shook out his clothes in protest and said to them, 'Your blood be on your own heads! I am clear of my responsibility. From now on I will go to the Gentiles'" (Acts 18:5-6).

Several years after his conversion, this initial call was renewed and confirmed by the church at Antioch where he had ministered for a year. "While they [the church leaders] were worshiping the Lord and fasting, the Holy Spirit said, 'Set apart for me Barnabas and Saul for the work to which I have called them'" (Acts 13:2). Thus the general call now became specific, and they joyously set out, "sent on their way by the Holy Spirit" (13:4).

The first major step in the fulfilling of the Lord's Great Commission and the beginning of the grand worldwide missionary enterprise had thus been safely negotiated.

THE RESHAPING OF AMBITION

A leader is usually an ambitious person. Even in his unregenerate days the apostle Paul had been fiercely ambitious, and conversion certainly did not quench the flame. He could not do things by halves, for there appeared to be an inner compulsion that drove him relentlessly forward. Impatient of the status quo, his gaze was always trained on greater achievements and distant horizons.

Paul's unregenerate ambition had previously focused on effacing the name of the impostor Jesus, exterminating his followers and quenching the growing influence of his church. His burning zeal for Judaism, which he considered the only true religion, drove him to wild excesses. Until the time of his dramatic conversion, "Saul was still breathing out murderous threats against the Lord's disciples" (Acts 9:1).

On several occasions Paul told of the fixated state of his heart at this pre-conversion stage: "I persecuted the followers of this Way to their death, arresting both men and women and throwing them into prison" (Acts 22:4). "Many a time I went from one synagogue to another to have them punished, and I tried to force them to blaspheme. In my obsession against them, I even went to foreign cities to persecute them" (Acts 26:11). "I was advancing in Judaism beyond many Jews my own age and was extremely zealous for the traditions of my fathers" (Galatians 1:14). These were the actions of a crazed man.

The superintending providence of God is further seen in the way this intense natural ambition was redirected into spiritually productive channels diametrically opposed to those of former days. His new ambition found a fresh center in the glory of Christ and the advancement of his kingdom. He nailed his old ambition to the cross, now longing to bring blessing to those whose extermination he had once plotted. "I long to see you," he wrote to the believers in Rome, "so that I may impart to you some spiritual gift to make you strong" (Romans 1:11).

Paul had two major ambitions. The first was to win the smile of the Lord. "So we make it our goal [our ambition] to please him" (2 Corinthians 5:9). Personal approval from Christ was his sufficient reward for any service or suffering. This ambition goaded him along the path of faithful though sacrificial service.

Paul's second ambition was related to his career: "It has always been my ambition to preach the gospel where Christ was not known, so that I would not be building on someone else's foundation" (Romans 15:20). It has been said that he suffered from acute spiritual claustrophobia—the fear of being confined in an enclosed space. He was in the grip of an insatiable passion for advance. He would not be fenced in. Had he not been called to go "far away to the Gentiles" (Acts 22:21)? He made it a point of honor to be true to his commission.

Paul of Tarsus was haunted by the regions beyond. His vision knew no horizons: Corinth, Rome, Spain. Kipling could have been speaking of Paul when he wrote:

> Something hidden, go and find it,
> Go and look behind the ranges,
> Something lost behind the ranges,
> Lost, and waiting for you—Go!

> God took care to hide that country,
> Till He judged his people ready.
> Then He chose me for His whisper,
> And I've found it, and it's yours.

Here as everywhere he was a model leader for the church in the coming ages. His missionary zeal fired Henry Martyn, who said that he desired "not to burn out for advance, to burn out for ambition, to burn out for self, but looking up at that whole burnt-offering, to burn out for God and His work." A similar ambition had fired the imagination and heart of every great missionary. Like Paul, we too should be ambitious to occupy every unoccupied field or territory for Christ.

It hardly needs to be emphasized that Paul's ambition was essentially selfless and Christ-centered. He was himself the best illustration of the disinterested love he advocated. He longed to be useful to God and his fellow men, and to discharge his debt to both. "Our hope is that . . . our area of activity among you will greatly expand, so that we can reach the gospel in the regions beyond you. For we do not want to boast about work already done in another man's territory" (2 Corinthians 10:15-16).

A NEW MOTIVATION

Only powerful motivation could inspire and maintain such a consuming ambition. In a number of incidental statements in his letters, the apostle revealed some of the motives that inspired his prodigious labors and made him the inspired and inspiring leader he became.

The first in point of time and in order of importance was Paul's unshakable conviction that *Christ is the promised Messiah,* thus having the right to the absolute lordship of Paul's life. The two questions he asked immediately after seeing the heavenly vision—"Who are you, Lord?" and "What shall I do, Lord?"—centered on these two facts (Acts 22:8, 10).

The second most important motive in Paul's changed life was the compelling power of *the love of Christ.* "For Christ's love compels us" (2 Corinthians 5:14)—it constrains us, controls us, leaves us no options. The love that had broken and captured his rebellious heart on the Damascus highway continued to hold him in willing vassalage until he met his Lord again in glory. It was this that nerved him for the incredible trials, sufferings, and privations that were his lot. This love for Christ inevitably found expression in the ardent love of those for whom he died.

Paul labored under an inescapable *sense of obligation.* "I

feel myself under a sort of universal obligation," he wrote, "I owe something to all men, from cultured Greek to ignorant savage" (Romans 1:13, PH). He had the authentic missionary passion to share a great discovery, and this all-embracing obligation overleapt all racial barriers, overrode all cultural differences. He felt himself equally indebted to *all men,* since all were included in the scope of Christ's love and sacrifice. Social status, wealth, poverty, and illiteracy were all irrelevant. At all costs Paul had to discharge his debt.

> Only like souls I see the folk thereunder,
>   Bound who should be conquerors,
>   Slaves who should be kings.
> Hearing their one hope with an empty wonder,
>   Sadly contented with a show of things.
> Then with a rush the intolerable craving
>   Shivers throughout me like a trumpet call,
> Oh, to save these, to perish for their saving,
>   Die for their life, be offered for them all.
>   —*F. W. H. Myers*

"*The fear of the Lord*" was to the apostle a solemn reality that constituted a powerful motivation leading him to seek the lost. "Since, then, we know what it is to fear the Lord, we try to persuade men" (2 Corinthians 5:11). He believed there was and is such a thing as the wrath of the God of love. "The wrath of God is being revealed from heaven against all the godlessness and wickedness of men who suppress the truth by their wickedness" (Romans 1:18).

But whenever Paul referred to the wrath and judgment of

God, he spoke in loving tones of the Savior's mercy. "The wages of sin is death, but the gift of God is eternal life in Christ Jesus our Lord" (Romans 6:23).

The hope of the return of Christ was to Paul a source of strong spiritual motivation. He was deeply influenced by the powers of the world to come. "Our citizenship is in heaven. And we eagerly await a Savior from there, the Lord Jesus Christ" (Philippians 3:20). This glorious prospect was to him a spur to his soul-winning endeavor. "What is our hope, our joy, or the crown in which we will glory in the presence of our Lord Jesus when he comes? Is it not you? Indeed, you are our glory and joy" (1 Thessalonians 2:19).

POSTGRADUATE COURSES

> We all need to go to Arabia to learn lessons like these. The Lord Himself was led up into the wilderness. And in one form or another, every soul who has done a great work in the world has passed through similar periods of obscurity, suffering, disappointment or solitude.
>
> —*F. B. Meyer*

Although the apostle Paul had enjoyed the advantage of a superb religious and academic training, before he could attain maximum usefulness in achieving God's eternal purpose for the Gentiles, he had to undertake a postgraduate course. His fiery spirit had to be tempered, and yet without any quenching of its zeal.

To achieve this, a period of withdrawal, of solitude was necessary, for solitude is an important element in the maturing process. Spiritual leadership does not develop best in the glare of publicity. Further, since God aims at quality in his chosen instruments, time is no object with him. We are always in a hurry, but he is not.

Unlike many people today, Paul did not rush immediately into his new work, but wisely sought solitude. He desired to be alone to meditate and to relate the present to the past. "I did not consult any man, nor did I go up to Jerusalem to see those who were apostles before I was, but I went immediately into Arabia and later returned to Damascus" (Galatians 1:16-17). Strangely, there is no mention in Luke's record in Acts of Paul's stay in Arabia.

Today there is an unhealthy tendency to push young converts into prominence before they have really found their feet. Paul avoided this snare. Probably as much as twelve years of quiet training and evangelistic endeavor elapsed before he launched upon his flaming missionary career.

The exact location of his years of retreat is not certain. Some think he went to Sinai—a reasonable conjecture. But Sir William Ramsay's view is that he went to the adjacent country to the east of Damascus.

The spiritual revolution in his life had been so devastating that he needed time to adjust his thinking. There, in the school of the Spirit—"a one-man seminary"—with infinite leisureliness God taught and trained the chosen messenger who was to open the world to the gospel. He had to review the whole course of Old Testament truth in the light of the new revelation that had come to him. Here was a demanding challenge in exegesis.

The far-reaching, undreamed of implications of the sufferings and death of the Messiah had to be thought through.

He now had to formulate his theology along radically different lines. Through these formative days and years, under the Spirit's tutelage, he was unconsciously storing his mind with facts and arguments that were to stand him in good stead in the coming days of controversy and opposition. There, too, he dropped the intolerable burden of Pharisaic law-keeping and embraced the doctrine of free, but costly grace.

> Through men whom worldlings count as fools,
>   Chosen of God, and not of man,
> Reared in Thy secret training schools,
>   Moves forward Thy eternal plan.
>
> And now, though hidden from our ken,
>   In Midian's desert, Sinai's hill,
> Spirit of God, Thou hast Thy men,
>   Waiting Thy time to do Thy will.
>
> When blazing out upon one night
>   Flashes the Pentecostal flame,
> May I be found with heart alight,
>   Burning to magnify Thy name.
>   —*Frank Houghton*

Following his period of seclusion in Arabia, Paul returned to Damascus (Galatians 1:17), and three years later went back to "the holy city." He desired primarily, through fellowship with Peter, to gain more firsthand knowledge about the Lord. Secondarily, he hoped to win the rabbis to the new movement. In this he was bitterly disappointed.

Paul said of this experience in Jerusalem:

"I fell into a trance and saw the Lord speaking. 'Quick!' He said to me. 'Leave Jerusalem immediately, because they will not accept your testimony about me.'

"'Lord,' I replied 'these men know that I went from one synagogue to another to imprison and beat those who believe in you. And when the blood of your martyr Stephen was shed, I stood there giving my approval and guarding the clothes of those who were killing him.'

"Then the Lord said to me, 'Go; I will send you far away to the Gentiles.'" (Acts 22:17-21)

After his short-term ministry in Damascus and Jerusalem, Paul returned to Tarsus where he remained for about eight years. How he filled those years is not very clear, but we can be sure he was actively propagating his newfound faith. That time of preparatory evangelism culminated in a year of rich experience in the church at Antioch under the guidance of Barnabas.

From this church as his center, Paul embarked to fulfill his life charter as apostle to the Gentile world. Important years they were, during which he underwent a great maturing and deepening of character. It should be noted by aspiring leaders that Paul proved himself and approved himself to his own home church and city before moving out as a spiritual pioneer into wider spheres of service.

The result of these years of obscurity was that "when he came forth to his work he had a message—unborrowed, original, fresh from God."

Notes

1. Pollock, John, *The Man Who Shook the World* (Wheaton: Victor Books, 1972), Preface.

2. Speer, Robert, *Paul, the All-round Man* (New York: Revell 1909), 102.

3. Meyer, Frederick B., *Paul* (London: Morgan & Scott, 1910), 34.

4. Jefferson, *The Character of Paul,* 19.

5. Sanders, J. Oswald, *Bible Men of Faith* (Chicago: Moody, 1966), 200.

6. *The Sunday School Times,* September 30, 1928, 397.

7. Macartney, Clarence, *The Greatest Men of the Bible* (New York: Abingdon, 1941), 14.

8. Meyer, F. B., *Paul,* 64.

3
PORTRAIT OF A LEADER

A man is not only what he owes to his parents,
friends and teachers, but a man is also what God has made him by
calling him to some particular ministry and by endowing him with
appropriate natural and spiritual gifts.

JOHN STOTT

Wherever he went, Paul stood out as a man of unusual authority and force of personality—a man who was every inch a leader. At a gathering of missionary leaders in Shanghai many years ago, D. E. Hoste, who succeeded Hudson Taylor as general director of the China Inland Mission, was asked his opinion as to what was the mark of a good leader. With his usual whimsical humor he replied, "If I wanted to discover whether I was a leader, I would look behind me to see who was following!"

Paul never lacked followers. His qualities of character irresistibly lifted him above his colleagues and associates. For example, when he and Barnabas set out on their first missionary journey, the order was "Barnabas and Paul." But before long, by sheer force of character he outstripped the older man, and we read of "Paul and Barnabas." To his credit, it appears that large-hearted Barnabas did not resent the leadership of his younger colleague.

The incident at Lystra where Paul and Barnabas were mistaken for the gods Hermes and Zeus provides an interesting sidelight (Acts 14:11-20). There was a myth that these two gods had visited some of the people in that very area, rewarding them for their hospitality by turning their humble hut into a palace. They pictured Zeus as a tall majestic figure and Hermes as his messenger and spokesman. The people concluded that the tall, paternal Barnabas was Zeus and the physically unimpressive Paul was Hermes.

Their conclusion reveals the difference between the oriental and the occidental outlook. As people of Western civilization, we would naturally visualize as leader the dynamic, energetic person. But the Eastern mind would more likely consider the leader to be the one who sat and allowed his subordinates to do the work. The names allocated to both Paul and Barnabas reflect this concept. At the same time their assessment of Paul as Hermes was an impressive tribute to the authority and persuasiveness of his speech. Despite his weakness, fear, and trembling (1 Corinthians 2:3), his words were accompanied by divine power.

How fickle the crowd is! Worshiped as a god one day, and stoned the next! "'The gods have come down to us in human form!' . . . They stoned Paul and dragged him outside the city" (Acts 14:11, 19).

PORTRAIT OF A LEADER

A MAN OF MANY DIMENSIONS

In the shipwreck on the way to Rome, when it seemed inevitable that all would be lost, it was Paul who stood out as the heroic figure (Acts 27:27-44). The apostolic prisoner commanded the captain! Such was his massive personality and moral authority that the whole crew obeyed his orders without question. When he stood on trial for his life before King Agrippa, it was the prisoner who sentenced the judge, rather than the judge sentencing the prisoner (Acts 26).

Paul did not exercise his authority in a harsh or arbitrary manner, but neither did he suffer fools gladly. He was reasonable, not overbearing. He expressed his own attitude concerning authority when he wrote to the Corinthians, "This is why I write these things when I am absent, that when I come I may not have to be harsh in my use of authority—the authority the Lord gave me for building you up, not for tearing you down" (2 Corinthians 13:10).

The apostle's leadership was not perfect, but it provides us with a tremendously encouraging and inspiring example of what it means to continue pressing toward maturity. A leader must be willing to develop himself on many levels and in many capacities, but with a unity of purpose.

Paul's conception of the leader in Christian work is reflected in the words he used to describe that role. The leader is a *steward* (1 Corinthians 4:1 KJV), a word meaning the manager of the resources of a household. He is also an *administrator* (1 Corinthians 12:28), a word signifying the helmsman who steers the ship, and thus one who directs the task. A Christian leader is an *overseer* (Acts 20:28), a word meaning guardian or protector. He is an *elder* (Acts 20:17), implying maturity of Christian experience. And he is also a *ruler* (Romans 12:8 KJV), one who stands before the people and leads them.

Of course, not every leader fills all these roles, but Paul's use of these descriptive words gives some indication of the complexity of the task, and the need for flexibility and adaptability in exercising it. The versatility that characterized his own leadership is demonstrated in the variety of tactics he employed in dealing with the problems of differing people and churches.

Sometimes Paul was kindly and paternal: "We were gentle among you, like a mother caring for her little children" (1 Thessalonians 2:7-8, 11-12). But when necessity demanded, he thundered: "I already gave you a warning when I was with you the second time. I now repeat it while absent: On my return I will not spare those who sinned earlier or any of the others" (2 Corinthians 13:2-3).

Often he was brotherly: "But, brothers, when we were torn away from you for a short time . . . out of our intense longing we made every effort to see you. For we wanted to come to you" (1 Thessalonians 2:17-18). Sometimes he used stinging sarcasm in the hope of bringing his spiritual siblings to a better state of mind: "Already you have all you want! Already you have become rich! You have become kings—and that without us! . . . We are fools for Christ, but you are so wise in Christ! We are weak but you are strong! You are honored, we are dishonored!" (1 Corinthians 4:8-10).

We can see in Paul's writings that he was playful: "Be that as it may, I have not been a burden to you. Yet, crafty fellow that I am, I caught you by trickery!" (2 Corinthians 12:16). At other times he gave generous praise: "For you, brothers, became imitators of God's churches in Judea. . . . You suffered from your own countrymen the same things those churches suffered from the Jews" (1 Thessalonians 2:14). He urged one church to emulate the generosity of another: "I am not commending you, but I want to test the sincerity of your love by comparing it with the earnestness of others" (2 Corinthians 8:8).[1]

There is no rigid uniformity in Paul's leadership method. The flexible approach he adopted usually proved to be far more acceptable and successful.

In training men for leadership, Paul, like his Master, focused on individuals as well as the crowds. He poured his life into a small number of men with leadership potential. He did not try to exert a cultic control over their minds, nor did he place his reliance on platform personality or elaborate public relations. His ultimate reliance was on the promised cooperation of the Holy Spirit.

The apostle's dynamic leadership left its impression on the whole Western world. As R. E. O. White said of Paul's influence, "Far beyond his own imagining, or the understanding of his contemporaries, Paul engraved his name deeply on the story of mankind as one of the makers of Europe, and indeed of the whole Western world; for the things he wrote and stood for became the unquestioned assumptions of the whole medieval way of life, upon which modern civilisation in the West was built."[2]

One striking feature of his leadership was that it did not wane with the passing of the years, nor could prison bars restrict its scope. Even when he was "Paul the aged," he remained the model and leader of a group of dynamic younger men. The affection he kindled in his followers' hearts was mirrored in the tears that flowed when he told them they would see him no more (Acts 20:36-38).

Sensitivity to Others

Leaders with the talents and force of character that Paul possessed frequently tend to overpower or override others less forceful, and to be insensitive to the rights and convictions of others. Paul was punctilious in his relationships, handling difficult situations with rare tact and consideration.

The original meaning of the word *tact* referred to the sense of touch, and came to mean skill in dealing with persons or sensitive situations. Tact is defined as "intuitive perception, especially a quick and fine perception of what is fit and proper and right." It alludes to one's ability to conduct delicate negotiations and personal matters in a way that recognizes mutual rights, and yet leads to a harmonious solution.

Paul was thoughtful and sensitive to the rights and feelings of others, and studiously avoided getting wires crossed. He took pains to avoid trespassing on another's sphere of authority. The following passage reveals his conception of territorial courtesy:

> We will not boast of authority we do not have. . . . It is not as though we were trying to claim credit for the work someone else has done among you. Instead, we hope that your faith will grow and that, still within the limits set for us, our work among you will be greatly enlarged. After that we will be able to go and preach the Good News to other cities that are far

beyond you, where no one else is working; then there will be no question about being in someone else's field (2 Corinthians 10:13-16 LB).

Paul's sensitivity is seen uniquely in the tactful manner in which he carried on negotiations with Philemon about Onesimus. "I did not want to do anything without your consent, so that any favor you do will be spontaneous and not forced" (Philemon 14).

THE COURAGE OF AN APOSTOLIC LION

The test of courage in a leader includes his ability to meet unpleasant or even devastating facts and situations without panic, as well as his willingness to take firm action when necessary, even if it is unpopular. "Because right is right, to follow right were wisdom in the fear of consequence."

Paul's moral courage matched his physical courage, which was a very high order. He was deterred neither by prospective suffering nor by present danger whenever he was conscious that they confronted him upon the path of duty. The tenacity of his courage is evident in his own words: "And now, compelled by the Spirit, I am going to Jerusalem, not knowing what will happen to me there. I only know that in every city the Holy Spirit warns me that prison and hardships are facing me" (Acts 20:22-23).

The brave apostle confronted the raging mob like a lion for his Master's sake. "Paul wanted to appear before the crowd, but the disciples would not let him. Even some of the officials of the province, friends of Paul, sent him a message begging

him not to venture into the theater" (Acts 19:30-31). He realized that it is not always our duty to avoid danger.

But this was not a courage that knew no fear. "I came to you
in weakness and fear, and with much trembling," he told the
Corinthians (1 Corinthians 2:3). A stolid indifference to danger is not a sign of true courage. The man who does not know
fear cannot know courage. Paul knew fear, but he also knew
that God had not given him a spirit of fear, but "a spirit of power" (2 Timothy 1:7).

Paul displayed to a remarkable degree that ideal balance
of mind, so esteemed by the Greeks, that veers neither to the
right nor to the left. His courage did not slip into rashness on
the one hand nor timidity on the other. His letters revealed
how fearlessly yet tenderly he grasped the nettle of a critical
situation, writing a difficult letter or administering a deserved
rebuke.

Paul was not prepared to allow things to go by default
merely to spare himself the heartbreak of an act of necessary
discipline. He displayed tremendous courage when as a com-
parative newcomer, he rebuked the great Peter for his pretense.
"When Peter came to Antioch, I opposed him to his face, because he was in the wrong" (Galatians 2:11).

THE DECISIVENESS OF A
FIELD COMMANDER

One of the seven essential ingredients of effective military
leadership laid down by Field Marshal Montgomery was, "He
must have the power of clear decision." The apostle Paul, as
a spiritual field commander, fully qualified in this category

PORTRAIT OF A LEADER

of leadership. Indeed this was a key feature of his character which he displayed at the very time of his conversion.

When the heavens burst open and he saw the exalted Christ, his first question was, "Who are you, Lord?" The answer, "I am Jesus of Nazareth, whom you are persecuting" (Acts 22:8), toppled his entire theological universe, but he immediately accepted the implications of his discovery. An absolute capitulation to the Son of God was the only possible response, and, with his newly completed soul, he decided on the spot that he needed to have unreserved allegiance and obedience. This led to his second question, "What shall I do, Lord?" (Acts 22:10).

Vacillation and indecision were foreign to Paul's training. Once he was sure of the facts, he moved to swift decision. To be granted light was to follow it. To see his duty was to do it. Once he is sure of the will of God, the effective leader will go into action regardless of consequences. He will be willing to burn his bridges behind him and accept responsibility for failure as well as for success.

Procrastination and vacillation are fatal to leadership. A sincere though mistaken decision is better than no decision. Indeed, no decision *is* a decision—a decision that the present situation is acceptable. In most decisions the difficulty is not in knowing what we ought to do, but in summoning the moral purpose to come to a decision about it. This resolution process was no problem to Paul.

THE GIVE-AND-TAKE OF ENCOURAGEMENT

Whether or not it was because of his earlier associations with Barnabas (meaning "Son of Encouragement," so named by his colleagues), Paul himself specialized in this ministry. Encouragement is a constantly recurring element in his letters to churches, especially those churches who were passing through fiery trials. Although he himself was so strong in character and faith, he was not exempt from discouragement or depression. He reached a high plane of triumph in Christian living, but he did not attain it overnight.

"God, who comforts the downcast, comforted us by the coming of Titus," Paul testified (2 Corinthians 7:6). He further claimed, *"I have learned to* be content whatever the circumstances" (Philippians 4:11). The implication is that this had not always been the case, but that he had at last mastered the secret of rising above discouraging circumstances. It had been a learning process with him, so we too can take courage.

> Let no one think that sudden in a moment
> All is accomplished and the work is done;
> Though with thy earliest dawn thou shouldst begin it
> Scarce were it ended by thy setting sun.
> —*F. W. H. Myers*

In the second letter to the Corinthians, in which he rejoices that his sterner, first letter had achieved its purpose, Paul shares with them some secrets he had learned that enabled him to rise above discouragement. Twice he uses the clause "we do not lose heart" (2 Corinthians 4:1, 16), and from the context we can glean the reason. In chapter 3, he had been describing the radiant glory of the new covenant of grace as compared with the old covenant of law, and then in 3:18 he had revealed the secret of sharing and reflecting that radiance.

Thus we can understand Paul's statements of spiritual stamina in chapter 4. "We do not lose heart" is a strong statement, which other translations highlight well: "we never give up" (LB); "we do not get discouraged" (AMP); "we never collapse." A strong motivation must always be present to achieve such a desirable end.

One reason Paul never lost heart was that he had been entrusted with a glorious ministry. "Therefore, since through God's mercy we have this ministry, we do not lose heart" (2 Corinthians 4:1).

Paul must have wondered at first if his misguided persecuting zeal had disqualified him for God's service. But he was reassured when he realized that he had "received mercy" (KJV), having been "entrusted with this commission" (NEB). He was not a self-confident, self-made man. He recognized that "our competence comes from God. He has made us competent as ministers of a new covenant" (2 Corinthians 3:5-6). He never got over the wonder that God trusted *him* so much.

Here was a revolutionary message to proclaim. It is difficult for us to realize how incredible it must have seemed to the Jews, for it was a complete reversal of the old covenant concept on which their whole religious life was based. The inexorable "thou shalt . . . thou shalt not" had been replaced by the divine undertaking—"I will . . . I will." The new covenant came with the assurance of divine enabling (Jeremiah 31:31-34, Ezekiel 36:25-29, Hebrews 8:8-13). It was not a message for a spiritual elite, but was tailored especially to meet the needs of people who had failed—a message especially for failures!

"When I have such a glorious message," said Paul, "no wonder I do not lose heart!" It is when we lose the sense of wonder at the message with which we have been entrusted that we lose heart.

Paul also had an assurance of being endowed with new divine strength every day. "Though outwardly we are wasting away, yet inwardly we are being renewed day by day" (2 Corinthians 4:16). In the midst of the wear and tear and suffering to which he was exposed, his body was indeed wasting away. But that was not the whole story: at the same time a counter-process was taking place. His inner being was experiencing spiritual renewal—fresh additions of strength from God. "No wonder we don't give up!" Paul exclaimed.

Our heavenly Father knows the strains and stresses involved in our service to Him. He is not insensitive to the cost at which we often carry it out. For He knows when we near the point of collapse, and to counteract this, He promises daily renewal. Why do we not appropriate more from God when there is such ample provision?

Paul was very susceptible to external influences and felt loneliness acutely, but news of the spiritual progress of individuals or churches greatly cheered and encouraged him. "Therefore, brothers, in all our distress and persecution we were encouraged about you because of your faith" (1 Thessalonians 3:7). He found that encouragement was a two-way thing.

FAITH AND VISION

It is one of the most important functions of a spiritual leader to communicate his own faith and vision to those who follow him. When Paul reckoned with God, he trusted *in depth*.

The apostle himself stated, "I have faith in God that it will happen just as he told me" (Acts 27:25).

James T. Dyet writes: "There was no credibility gap with God as far as Paul was concerned. The faith in God's word which Paul displayed on the high seas was typical of the confidence he had in Him to do everything He promised."[3]

Paul was nothing if not a man of faith. His trust in Christ was absolute, and wherever he went he left behind him people whose faith had been quickened and renewed. He saw faith as the driving principle of the Christian's daily life. "We live by faith, not by sight" (2 Corinthians 5:7).

Paul regarded the craving for outward signs or miracles, or for inward feelings in order to bolster faith, as a sign of spiritual immaturity. Faith is occupied with the invisible and spiritual. Sight is concerned with the visible and tangible. Sight concedes reality only to things present and seen. "Faith forms a solid ground for what is hoped for, a conviction of unseen realities" (Hebrews 11:1, Berkeley).

Faith is confidence, reliance, trust, and has its dealings directly with God. Indeed, "Without faith it is impossible to please God." (Hebrews 11:6). Paul's faith in God was a childlike, effortless trust that was never betrayed. With such a God as revealed by Scripture, he was as much at home in the realm of the impossible as in that of the possible. His God knew no limitations, and therefore he was worthy of limitless trust.

It was Paul who told us that "faith comes from hearing the message, and the message is heard through the word of Christ" (Romans 10:17). True faith does not come through introspection, but through a sincere involvement in what God has said.

If we desire to have faith, we must first discover a divinely authenticated fact on which it can rest. Paul reminds us that this was the secret of the father of the faithful, Abraham. "He did not waver through unbelief regarding the promise of God, but was strengthened in his faith and gave glory to God" (Romans 4:20). Faith feeds on the pledged word of God.

Faith is vision. Paul was able to see things that were invisible to many of his more earthbound colleagues. Elisha's servant saw clearly the vastness of the enemy's encircling army, but Elisha's faith enabled him to see the invincible and environing hosts of heaven (2 Kings 6). His faith imparted vision.

Where others saw difficulties, Paul saw opportunities. "I will stay on at Ephesus until Pentecost, because a great door for effective work has opened to me, and there are many who oppose me" (1 Corinthians 16:8-9). So far from deterring him, great opposition acted only as a stimulus to enter the open door.

Although essentially a realist, Paul was no less an optimist. No pessimist ever made an inspiring leader. The man who sees the *difficulties* so narrowly that he does not discern the *possibilities* will never inspire others. Paul would fit Browning's description:

> One who has never turned his back,
> But marched breast-forward,
> Never doubting clouds would break,
> Never dreamed, though right were worsted,
> Wrong would triumph.

THE VALUE OF FRIENDSHIP

"You can tell a man by his friends." There is more than a grain of truth in this adage. A man's ability to make and maintain enduring friendships will in general be the measure of his ability to lead.

Unlike many other great men, such as General de Gaulle, Paul's was not the greatness of isolation. He was essentially gregarious, and possessed in a unique degree the power of capturing and holding the intense love and loyalty of the friends with whom he freely mixed. His love for them was genuine and ran deep.

Paul was seldom found working alone. He became desperately lonely when isolated. "He had a genius for friendship," wrote Harrington C. Lees. "No man in the New Testament made fiercer enemies, but few men in the world have had better friends. They cluster around him so thickly that we are apt to lose their personality in their devotion."[4]

His happiness was always heightened by the presence of his friends. He did his best work when accompanied by trusted fellow workers.

Inevitably Paul involved his friends in all sorts of risks for Christ's sake, but they followed him cheerfully, because they were assured of his love and concern for them. His letters glow with the warmth of his affection and appreciation of his fellow workers.

It was John R. Mott's counsel to "rule by the heart. When argument and logic and other forms of persuasion fail, fall back on the heart—genuine friendship." Personal friendliness will do more to draw the best out of other people than prolonged and even successful argument. Paul was a master of this art.

"Nothing can take the place of affection," wrote A. W. Tozer in his biography of R. A. Jaffray. "Those who have it in generous measure have a magic power over men."

> Hearts I have won, of sister or of brother,
> Quick on earth, or buried in the sod,
> Lo, every heart awaiteth me, another
> Friend in the blameless family of God.
> —*F. W. H. Myers*

One great secret of Paul's friendships was his capacity to love unselfishly, even if his love was met with nothing in return. "So I will very gladly spend for you everything I have and expend myself as well. I love you more, will you love me less?" (2 Corinthians 12:15).

Luke, the beloved physician, a man who hazarded his life with his friend Paul is an example of intimacy between men of similar age and tastes. Paul's friendship with Barnabas was also very warm and, happily, outlived their acute difference of opinion over the defection of John Mark.

Paul's friendship with Timothy is a model of friendship between an older and a younger man. Many women, too, were numbered among the friends whom he remembered with affection (Romans 16). The apostle's capacity for friendship was a prime factor in his ability to reproduce himself in Christian leadership.

A Confident Modesty

In his preaching and writing, Paul unselfconsciously used his own experiences as illustrations, and shared his own inner battles, frustrations, and failures. He did not denigrate his own sincerity and integrity (2 Corinthians 1:23, Romans 9:1-2), but neither did he exalt himself unduly. "For by the grace given me I say to every one of you: Do not think of yourself more highly than you ought, but rather think of yourself with sober judgment, in accordance with the measure of faith God has given you" (Romans 12:3).

Paul was fully conscious of his own failures and shortcomings, especially since his standard was a maturity measured by "the whole measure of the fullness of Christ" (Ephesians 4:13). He confessed to the limitation of his own attainment. "Not that I have already obtained all this, or have already been made perfect, but I press on to take hold of that for which Christ Jesus took hold of me" (Philippians 3:12). But instead of discouraging him from further moral endeavors, it only caused him to strain "toward what is ahead."

Several of his incidental sayings reflect his self-image:

What is Paul? Only [a servant], through whom you came to believe. (1 Corinthians 3:5)

I came to you in weakness and fear, and with much trembling. (1 Corinthians 2:3)

ORT

> When I preach the gospel, I cannot boast, for I am compelled to preach . . . . I am simply discharging the trust committed to me. (1 Corinthians 9:16-17)

> Not that we are competent in ourselves to claim anything for ourselves, but our competence comes from God. (2 Corinthians 3:5)

And yet, with all this very modest (though not morbid) self-appraisal, Paul daringly exhorts the Corinthians, "Therefore I urge you to imitate me" (1 Corinthians 4:16). But later in the epistle he adds an important rider: "Follow my example, *as I follow the example of Christ*" (1 Corinthians 11:1). Holding up his life as an example was not an exhibition of pride, for what he was and what he had achieved had been done by Christ. "I will not venture to speak of anything except what Christ has accomplished through me" (Romans 15:18).

> Aye, for this Paul, a scorn and a despising,
> Weak as you know him and the wretch you see,
> Even in these eyes shall ye behold him rising,
> Strength in infirmities and Christ in me.
> —*F. W. H. Myers*

Paul knew his own worth and would not allow his denigrators to underestimate him. "I may not be a trained speaker, but I do have knowledge. We have made this perfectly clear to you in every way" (2 Corinthians 11:6).

Sometimes, although it was distasteful to him, he felt compelled to "boast" in defense of his apostolic office, but he usually accompanied it with an apology. "What anyone else dares to boast about . . . I also dare to boast about . . . . If I must boast, I will boast of the things that show my weakness . . . . Even if I should choose to boast, I would not be a fool, because I would be speaking the truth" (2 Corinthians 11:21, 30; 12:6). It was only with reluctance that he spoke of his many sufferings (2 Corinthians 11:21-33). This delicate but wholesome balance between undue self-deprecation and self-exaltation serves as a wonderful model for the Christian leader.

Paul was quite generous in his appraisal of others, and was totally free of envying their spiritual success or gifts. He delighted to associate fellow workers with himself, even young ones, on terns of *equality*. "We are God's fellow workers" (1 Corinthians 3:9).

Speaking of Timothy, he wrote, "If Timothy comes, see to it that he has nothing to fear . . . for he is carrying on the work of the Lord, just as I am" (1 Corinthians 16:10). He referred to Titus as his "partner" (2 Corinthians 8:23). It is small wonder that these younger men, to whom he freely delegated responsibility and respect, would have done anything for him.

A PROGRESSIVE HUMILITY

Humility is not included in the prospectus of the world's leadership courses, where prominence, publicity, and self-advertisement loom large. It should not be so among us, according to Jesus. "Instead, whoever wants to become great among you must be your servant" (Mark 10:43). Paul followed closely in the steps of his Lord in this respect. "Paul had none of the self-will, the exclusive assertiveness of the consciously great man."[5]

The apostle who was highly esteemed by others lived in the humility of a great repentance. While he did not morbidly dwell on it, he never forgot that he had ruthlessly persecuted the church of God. And when his enemies said he was not fit to live, he did not dispute their assessment. An ever-present sense of indebtedness caused him to have a humble self-image. He had no desire to have a reputation higher than he had earned. "Even if I should choose to boast, I would not be a fool, because I would be speaking the truth. But I refrain, so no one will think more of me than is warranted by what I do or say" (2 Corinthians 12:6).

Paul warned the Colossian Christians to beware of a self-conscious, ascetic humility, which is really the subtlest form of pride. "Do not let anyone who delights in false humility and the worship of angels disqualify you for the prize . . . . He has lost connection with the Head . . ." (Colossians 2:18-19).

Paul's humility was a progressive quality, deepening with the passing years. Regard his own words:

> I am the least of the apostles and do not even deserve to be called an apostle. (1 Corinthians 15:9)

> Although I am less than the least of all God's people, this grace was given me: to preach to the Gentiles the unsearchable riches of Christ. (Ephesians 3:8)

> Christ Jesus came into the world to save sinners—of whom I am the worst. (1 Timothy 1:15)

Although he was genuinely humble and without false modesty, Paul was not at all backward when it came to defending his apostolic office and authority. "I am afraid that . . . your minds may somehow be led astray from your sincere and pure devotion to Christ. For if someone comes to you and preaches a Jesus other than the Jesus we preached . . . you put up with it easily enough. But I do not think I am in the least inferior to those 'super-apostles'" (2 Corinthians 11:3-5). One constantly marvels at the sane balance Paul exercised in very sensitive areas.

A WAY WITH THE WRITTEN WORD

In any leadership position, the ability to communicate clearly and effectively, whether in correspondence or in other literary work is a quality much to be desired. Where it is lacking, misunderstandings very quickly arise. Paul, as in so many other areas, was a master of this art. Whether his letters were written in the midst of a busy itinerant ministry or from the unwelcome solitude of his prison cell, he succeeded in injecting his personality very vividly into his writing.

It is in the unstudied correspondence that we reveal our true selves, and in his letters the real Paul peers out from every page. We know more of the man from his letters than from any other historical source. They are models for any Christian leader, combining as they do clarity of thought and felicity of expression. They reveal keen spiritual insight coupled with sound common sense and loving concern.

The rich profusion of thought and the excitement of the truth Paul wished to convey sometimes caused him to break his train of thought or leave sentences unfinished. In the early days of the church, Irenaeus defended Paul because he "frequently uses a transposed order in his sentences, due to the rapidity of his discourses, and the impetus of the Spirit who is in him."

Not all of his letters were pleasant and easy to write. Indeed, in Paul's second letter to the Corinthians, he referred to his previous letter which contained exhortation and extreme rebuke. "I wrote you out of great distress and anguish of heart and with many tears, not to grieve you but to let you know the depth of my love for you" (2 Corinthians 2:4).

When Paul had a difficult letter to write, he was careful to dip his pen in tears, not in acid. After he had written his strong letter to the erring Corinthians, his tender pastor's heart caused him to wonder whether he had been too severe. He could not rest for anxiety, lest they should misunderstand what he had written. "Even if I caused you sorrow by my letter," he wrote afterward, "I do not regret it. Though I did regret it—I see that my letter hurt you, but only for a little while—yet now I am happy, not because you were made sorry, but because your sorrow led you to repentance. For you became sorrowful as God intended and so were not harmed in any way by us" (2 Corinthians 7:8-9).

In writing a letter of this nature, Paul's objective was not to win an argument, but to resolve a spiritual problem, restore harmony and unity, and produce a growing maturity. From him we can learn that, while it is important to couch our letters in clear speech so that the meaning is plain, it is even more important that they breathe a spirit of loving concern.

Letters are a relatively unsatisfactory medium of communication. They cannot smile, and they have no eyes to express love when they are saying something difficult. We should therefore take extra care to see that they are warm in tone. When a very special friend of mine wrote letters that could have caused hurt feelings, he made a practice of holding them overnight, reading them again in the morning to make sure that the tone and spirit were right.

Encouragement and inspiration abounded in Paul's correspondence. He always aimed at the spiritual enrichment of the recipients, but that did not mean that he refrained from faithful correction and rebuke when they were called for. "Have I now become your enemy by telling you the truth?" he asked the Galatian believers? "My dear children, for whom I am again in the pains of childbirth until Christ is formed in you, how I wish I could be with you now and change my tone, because I am perplexed about you!" (Galatians 4:16, 19-20).

Letters were an important part of Paul's follow-up program, contributing greatly to the growth and development of the churches he wrote to. George Whitefield, the silver-tongued evangelist, emulated Paul in this area. It was said that after preaching to large crowds, he would often sit up until three o'clock in the morning writing letters of instruction and encouragement to new converts.

No one would have been more surprised than Paul had someone told him that his pastoral letters would become one of the most influential forces in the religious and intellectual history of the world. They were written as part of his ordinary day's work, with "no thought of fame or futurity." Although they are not formal treatises and at times lack literary polish, Paul's letters have an eloquence and appeal of their own. Their influence through the ages cannot be estimated.

Tolstoy adds another thought: "How strange and odd it

would have seemed to the educated Romans of the middle of the first century that the letters addressed by a wandering Jew to his friends and pupils would have a hundred, a thousand, a hundred thousand times more readers and more circulation than all the poems, odes and elegies and elegant epistles of the authors of those days—and yet this is what has happened."

THE ART OF LISTENING

An aspiring politician approached Oliver Wendell Holmes and asked him how to get elected to office. He replied, "To be able to listen to others in a sympathetic and understanding manner is, perhaps, the most effective mechanism in the world for getting along with people, and tying up their friendship for good. Too few people practice the 'white magic' of being good listeners."

A missionary once spoke to me about his supervisor. "He doesn't listen to me," he complained. "Before I have a chance to really state the problem, he is giving the answer." This is the failing of the compulsive talker: he is afraid of a moment's silence. But the art of listening to one's colleagues must be mastered if the leader is to get at the root of the problems to be solved. Otherwise he will be likely to deal only with the symptom while the dire malady remains untreated.

When he was canvassing for votes at the time that Singapore was traveling toward independence, Lee Kuan Yew, who later became prime minister of the republic, spent every Saturday afternoon and evening in a different one of the fifty-one electoral precincts. He invited any citizen with problems to meet him and tell him his problem. He listened patiently to the woes of his people, and wherever possible he endeavored to secure redress. And the result? He was re-elected in every one of the precincts. He believed in and practiced the therapy of listening, and reaped the reward. A sympathetic ear is an invaluable asset.

Listening is a genuine attempt to understand what the other person desires to unload, done without prejudging the issue. A problem is often half-answered when it is brought out into the open and shared with a sympathetic listener. One missionary who became a casualty moaned, "If only he had listened to me! I needed someone with whom to share my problem."

Sensitivity to the needs of others is better expressed by listening than by talking. Leaders too frequently convey the impression, unconsciously and certainly unintentionally, that they are too busy to listen. In such a case, the leader and the colleague are both the losers. Happy is the leader who, in the midst of pressing duties, gives the impression that there is ample time to share the problem. He is the one who is most likely to provide a solution. Time spent listening is not time wasted.

Writing of Napoleon, D. E. Hoste said, "He was a good listener and possessed in a high degree the gift of applying the special knowledge of others to a particular set of circumstances. Doesn't history show that every truly great man is more or less made on these lines?"[6]

Reading between the lines, it is not difficult to sense that Paul was a man who knew the value of listening. When the people in the church of Corinth were floundering amid a jumble of problems for which they had no solution they knew they would find an understanding heart and a listening ear in Paul. His first letter was his answer to them.

A Generous and Broad-Minded Man

The transforming miracle of conversion is seldom more strikingly illustrated than in the case of Paul. The man who rushed down the Damascus road on his gruesome mission was a fanatical bigot with a closed mind. The blinded man who was led back to Damascus at last had within him the making of a generous and broad-minded saint. The narrow-minded Pharisee would go to any length to destroy the church. The broad-minded Christian would now go to any length to defend it and extend it.

Wherein lay the change? Not only had Paul seen the living Christ, but Christ now dwelt in his heart, immeasurably enlarging it and widening its horizons. The Spirit of God had poured the boundless love of God into his heart (Romans 5:5), and so the bigot became tolerant.

When some of his implacable opponents were preaching Christ "out of envy and rivalry. . . supposing that they [could] stir up trouble" (Philippians 1:15-17), it would have been very easy for the Paul of old to have hurled blistering denunciations at them. But the new Paul said, "But what does it matter? The important thing is that in every way, whether from false motives or true, Christ is preached. And because of this I rejoice" (1:18). Despite his great flexibility, it should be emphasized that Paul was not so tolerant as to compromise the essential truths of the faith, nor was he so broad as to be shallow.

The Necessity of Patience

Was John Chrysostom wrong in his judgment when he called patience the queen of virtues? Our usage of the word is too negative and passive to convey the rich meaning of the word Paul used so frequently.

William Barclay has invested the word *patience* with a very full and attractive significance. He comments on the word as used in this passage—"Add to your faith virtue; and to virtue knowledge; and to knowledge temperance; and to temperance *patience*" (2 Peter 1:5-6 KJV).

> The word never means the spirit that sits with folded hands and simply bears things. It is victorious endurance, masculine constancy under trial. It is Christian steadfastness, the brave and courageous acceptance of everything life can do to us, and the transmuting of even the worst into another step on the upward way. It is the courageous and triumphant ability to bear things, which enables a man to pass breaking point and not break, and always to greet the unseen with a cheer.[7]

Professor Barclay could have been drawing a word picture of the apostle, so fully does he illustrate the quality Paul is commending.

The quality or virtue of patience is essential, especially in relations with people. It is here that most of us break down. Paul lost out at this point in his disagreement with Barnabas (Acts 15:36-40), and also when he spoke disrespectfully to the high priest (Acts 23:1-5). But these were rare exceptions, not the rule.

The man who is impatient with the weaknesses and failures of others will be defective in leadership. "We who are strong ought to bear with the failings of the weak" (Romans 15:1). The good leader knows how to adapt his pace to that of his slower brother.

Patience is essential, especially when we seek to lead by persuasion rather than by command. It is not always easy to bring another to see your viewpoint and act accordingly, but there is great value in cultivating the art of persuasion that allows the individual to make his own decision.

> One life is like the dial of a clock.
> The hands are God's hands passing o'er and o'er,
> The short hand is the hand of Discipline;
> The long, the Hand of Mercy evermore.

> Slowly and surely discipline must pass,
> And God speaks at each stroke His Word of Grace,
> But ever on the hand of mercy moves,
> With blessing sixty-fold the trials efface.

> Each moment counts a blessing from our God,
> Each hour a lesson in the school of love,
> Both hands are fastened to a pivot sure,
> The great unchanging heart of God above.
> —*S. M. Zwemer*

THE DRIVING FORCE OF SELF-DISCIPLINE

A leader is able to lead others only because he disciplines himself. The person who does not know how to bow to discipline imposed from without, who does not know how to obey, will not make a good leader—nor will the one who has not learned to impose discipline within his own life. Those who scorn scripturally or legally constituted authority, or rebel against it, rarely qualify for high leadership positions.

> The heights of great men reached and kept
> Were not attained by sudden flight,
> But they, while their companions slept,
> Were toiling upward in the night.

Paul imposed on himself a rigorous inner discipline in two areas:

He *waged war with his body.* "I do not run like a man running aimlessly; I do not fight like a man beating the air. No, I beat my body and make it my slave so that after I have preached to others, I myself will not be disqualified for the prize" (1 Corinthians 9:26-27).

Here Paul was expressing a genuine fear, a real possibility. He had not yet completed the course. Even his vast experience and great successes did not render him immune to the subtle temptations of the body. In order that his ministry should not be short-circuited, he was willing to bring his bodily appetites under a self-discipline as strict as that of the Spartan athletes in the arena.

> Well let me sin, but not with my consenting,
> Well let me die, but willing to be whole:
> Never, O Christ—so stay me from relenting—
> Shall there be truce betwixt my flesh and soul.
> —*F. W. H. Myers*

The Christian leader is open to the danger of being defeated through overindulgence of physical appetites or through laziness. Such an acute danger calls for stern self-discipline. At the other end of the scale is an excess of physical activity which can lead to fatigue and exhaustion. The leader must be prepared to work even harder than his colleagues. But an exhausted man easily falls prey to the adversary. We should be alert to guard against both of these dangers.

He *waged war with his thoughts*. "The weapons we fight with are not the weapons of the world. On the contrary, they have divine power to demolish strongholds. We demolish arguments and every pretension that sets itself up against the knowledge of God, and we take captive every thought to make it obedient to Christ" (2 Corinthians 10:4-5).

Paul knew that sin has its genesis in the thought life, so he made it his constant endeavor to prevent his thoughts from wandering and to bring them under the control of Christ.

More than strong willpower is needed to bring and keep both body and mind under divine control. But God has made provision for this additional capacity. "The fruit of the Spirit is . . . *self-control*" (Galatians 5:22-23). Paul's secret was that he was "full of the Spirit," and thus desirable spiritual fruit was produced abundantly in his life.

SINCERITY AND INTEGRITY

In his letters, Paul laid himself bare as few would be willing to do, and in so doing he left the impression of an utterly sincere man. During World War II, the young Billy Graham was invited by Sir Winston Churchill to meet him in the Parliament buildings in London. When the young preacher was ushered into a large room, to his dismay he found himself in the presence of the whole British Cabinet. Churchill soon put him at ease, and Billy had the opportunity of sharing his faith. After he had left the room, Churchill remarked to his colleagues, "There goes a sincere man." Sincerity is an unconscious quality that is self-revealing.

Even before Paul's conversion, this quality of sincerity was manifest within him. "I thank God, whom I serve, as my forefathers did, with a clear conscience" (2 Timothy 1:3). Throughout his life, Paul was ingenuously conscious of his own integrity, and so he worked diligently at maintaining it. "So I strive always to keep my conscience clear before God and man" (Acts 24:16). He was just as sincere in building up the church as he was in trying to destroy it. Although he was desperately wrong in his days as inquisitor, he did not compromise his conscience, misguided as it was.

Paul did not shrink from God's scrutiny, and thus he could say, "My conscience is clear." Yet he hastened to add, "But that does not make me innocent. It is the Lord who judges me" (1 Corinthians 4:4). The apostle appealed to God to attest his sincerity. "Unlike so many, we do not peddle the word of God for profit. On the contrary, in Christ we speak before God with sincerity, like men sent from God" (2 Corinthians 2:17).

SPIRITUAL WISDOM

When men were to be selected for a subordinate leadership position within the church, one of the two prerequisite qualities specified was *wisdom*—an essential element for good leadership. "Brothers, choose seven men from among you who are known to be full of the Spirit and wisdom" (Acts 6:3).

True wisdom is more than knowledge, which is the basic accumulation of facts. It is more than mere intellectual acumen.

It is heavenly insight. Spiritual wisdom involves the knowledge of God and the intricacies of the human heart. It involves the right application of knowledge in moral and spiritual matters and in meeting perplexing situations and complex human relationships. Wisdom is a quality that restrains a leader from rash or eccentric action, imparting a necessary balance.

> Knowledge and wisdom, far from being one,
> Have of times no connection. Knowledge dwells
> In heads replete with thoughts of other men:
> Wisdom, in minds attentive to their own.
> Knowledge is proud that he has learned so much,
> Wisdom is humble, that he knows no more.

The high place Paul gave to spiritual wisdom is seen in the way he constantly contrasted it with the vaunted wisdom of the world. "Do not deceive yourselves. If any one of you thinks he is wise by standards of this age, he should become a 'fool' so that he may become wise. For the wisdom of this world is foolishness in God's sight" (1 Corinthians 3:18-19).

Wisdom was a frequent petition Paul raised in prayer for his converts and churches. "We have not stopped praying for you and asking God to fill you with the knowledge of his will through all spiritual wisdom and understanding" (Colossians 1:9).

Wisdom characterized the intentional method of Paul's preaching. "We proclaim [Christ], admonishing and teaching everyone with all wisdom, so that we may present everyone perfect in Christ" (Colossians 1:28). Wisdom inevitably characterizes the ministry of the Spirit-filled leader. "Let the word of Christ dwell in you richly as you teach and admonish one another with all wisdom" (Colossians 3:16).

To Paul we owe the revelation that "Christ Jesus . . . has become for us wisdom from God" (1 Corinthians 1:30).

ZEAL AND INTENSITY

Like his Master, Paul was wholehearted and zealous in all his work for God. The family of our Lord, as they observed his intense zeal, "went to take charge of him, for they said, 'He is out of his mind'" (Mark 3:21).

King Festus said the same of Paul. "At this point Festus interrupted Paul's defense. 'You are out of your mind, Paul!' he shouted. 'Your great learning is driving you insane'" (Acts 26:24). The worldly mind equates zeal for God with insanity, but in God's sight it is the highest form of wisdom.

> As to Thy last apostle's heart
> Thy lightning glance did then impart
> Zeal's never-dying fire.
>
> —*John Keble*

As he spoke to the crowd at the temple of his unregenerate days, Paul claimed, "Under Gamaliel I was thoroughly trained in the law . . . and was just as zealous for God as any of you are today" (Acts 22:3). But his early zeal led him into the terrible excesses which were later to be his greatest grief.

Paul's former intensity carried over into his Christian life, but the Spirit directed it into new and vastly productive channels. The word *zeal* refers to something within that "boils up"—the enthusiasm that irresistibly bubbles up in the heart.

When the disciples saw their Master in the temple, ablaze with holy zeal and flaming with sinless anger, they were astounded at this display of intense zeal, until they "remembered that it is written: 'Zeal for your house will consume me'" (John 2:17, Psalm 69:9).

In this quality Paul sought to imitate his Lord. A perusal of his letters and discourses reveals that the ideal he entertained for his converts was *a mind aflame with the truth of God, a heart ablaze with the love of God, and a will fired with a passion for the glory of God.*

It was the absence of these qualities that brought our Lord's solemn words to the church of Laodicea (Revelation 3:14-22). Such a charge could not be laid at Paul's door. It is the zealous, enthusiastic leader who most deeply and permanently impresses his followers.

Paul incidentally reveals the secret of his unabating zeal in Romans 12:11, which Archbishop H. C. Lees renders, "Not slothful in business; kept at boiling-point by the Holy Spirit, doing bondservice for the Master." The Holy Spirit is the central furnace that maintains our intensity and zeal. In all of us there is a subtle tendency to "cool off," and so we constantly need this warming ministry of the Holy Spirit, who kindles the fuel we feed to the fire.

When he entered the Interpreter's house, John Bunyan's Christian was perplexed as he observed a man pouring water on the fire, for the flames only leapt higher. His mystification was dispelled when he saw at the back of the fire another man pouring oil on the flames. In a world where there are all too many people ready to pour cold water, the oil-on-the-fire of *zeal* is a gracious and rare ministry—"kept at boiling point by the Holy Spirit."

> I saw a human life ablaze for God,
>   I felt a power divine
> As through a vessel of frail clay
>   I saw God's glory shine.
> Then woke I from a dream
>   And cried aloud,
> My Father, give to me
>   The blessing of a life consumed,
>   That I may live for Thee.

Notes

1. Speer, Robert, *The Man Paul* (London: S.W. Partridge), 289.

2. White, Reginald E. O., *Apostle Extraordinary* (London: Pickerings, 1962).

3. Dyet, James T., *Man of Steel and Man of Velvet* (Denver: Accent Books, 1976), 55.

4. Lees, Harrington C., *St. Paul and His Friends* (London: Robert Scott) 11.

5. *Paul, the All-round Man,* 124.

6. Thompson, Phyllis, *D. E. Hoste* (London: Lutterworth) 157.

7. Barclay, William, *Letters of Peter and Jude* (Edinburgh: St. Andrews Press), 258.

4

AN EXALTED VIEW OF GOD

What comes to our minds when we think of God
is the most important thing about us.

A. W. TOZER

The apostle Paul's conception of God significantly shaped his theology and motivated his service. It was fundamental to the nature of his leadership. As J. B. Phillips demonstrated in his book *Your God Is Too Small,* an inadequate view of God will limit and adversely affect all we attempt to do.

Paul's faith was built on the doctrine of the Trinity. The Apostle's Creed would be a summary of the crucial tenets of his faith, which was essentially trinitarian. "I believe in God the Father Almighty . . . and in Jesus Christ his only Son, our Lord . . . . I believe in the Holy Spirit." He conceived of "God in the sublime majesty of His Being as one God in three Persons. Within the unity of His Being there is a distinction of 'Persons' whom we call the Father the Son and the Holy Spirit."[1]

To Paul, God was the great Reality, and he felt no necessity to argue for his existence. His was a God who was sovereign in power, but sympathetic toward human frailty and solicitous for human welfare. Life without God was inconceivable.

Paul's ideas of God were shaped by the Old Testament records of God's dealings with his people. Thus he had no problem believing in the supernatural, for the Hebrew chronicles of the miraculous were staggering.

One way to discover Paul's conception of God is to study the methods by which he sought to strengthen the hands of his young protégés, Timothy and Titus, for their demanding service. This brand of spiritual nurturing is a valuable lesson in leadership for us all. *Paul aimed to show his spiritual apprentices a greater God,* impressing them with the grandeur and majesty of the One they were privileged to serve.

The various titles for God which Paul employed in his pastoral letters served in a unique way to reveal some fresh facets of God's greatness and glory. Let's consider some of the titles of God that shaped Paul's theology and directed his actions.

Paul acclaims the good news of Jesus Christ as "the glorious gospel of *the blessed God*" (1 Timothy 1:11). Rotherham felicitously translates it, "the gospel of the glory of *the happy God.*" This rather beatific title describes God not as One who is the object of blessing, but as One who enjoys in himself the fullness of joy. He lives in the sublime atmosphere of his own eternal happiness (Hebrews 1:9). Jesus himself possesses a surplus of joy that He has bequeathed to His disciples, a storehouse which can supply us with unique blessings for our lives.

The title "blessed" is applied to God for two reasons: (1) He is entirely *self-sufficient.* We are constantly striving to become what we are not, in order to supply what we lack. God needs nothing and no one to complement Him. (2) He is *absolute perfection.* The sum total of all virtues is resident in Him. He is the God of all blessedness, in whom nothing is lacking or in excess. Thus Paul encourages Timothy to believe that the gospel he is to preach arises out of an environment of joy—the happy heart of God, which is perpetually overflowing.

"THE KING ETERNAL, IMMORTAL, INVISIBLE, THE ONLY GOD"

Immediately after Paul surveyed God's amazing grace to "the worst" of sinners—himself—he spontaneously burst into a doxology that unveils the nature and attributes of God, giving us unique glimpses of His glory. "Now to the King eternal, immortal, invisible, the only God, be honor and glory for ever and ever" (1 Timothy 1:17). Let's take a closer look one by one at these words used by Paul to describe his beloved God.

"The king of all the ages" (1 Timothy 1:17 PH)—Man is a creature of time, bound by clocks and calendars, but God is King of all worlds and all ages. His power and sovereignty are demonstrated in every epoch. He is the absolute Ruler of time.

God uses those who try to destroy His church to build it. He overrules evil for good. He moves with infinite ease through the ages toward the fulfillment of His eternal purpose. Paul described God's providence in the lives of all mankind when he said, "He fixed the epochs of their history and the limits of their territory" (Acts 17:26 NEB). God directs the events of each era of world history to its appointed goal. He weaves out of seemingly contradictory events a harmonious and beautiful pattern reflecting His own perfection.

"Immortal"—Only God is fully incorruptible, imperishable, not subject to the aging process of time and change, decay and death. Immortality is a part of God's very essence, whereas immortality is given to us only as a gift, derived from Him. God never changes (Malachi 3:6).

"Invisible"—No immediate and full vision of God is possible to man, for God has chosen to remain unseen except in Christ, who said, "Anyone who has seen me has seen the Father" (John 14:9)—and even then we see God only by faith. In Christ we can now see the One who is essentially invisible (John 1:18). The finite can never fully comprehend the infinite. Even Moses saw only the afterglow when God passed by (Exodus 33:22-23).

"The only God"—Our God is indeed the only God—not just numerically, but uniquely. There is no other like Him. "To whom will you compare me? Or who is my *equal?*" He asks (Isaiah 40:25). He is solitary, yet not aloof or isolated, as were the Greek gods.

"KING OF KINGS AND LORD OF LORDS"

"The Living God" (1 Timothy 3:15)—It was this quality that distinguished Israel's God from the heathen gods. The church Paul endeavored to serve was not a temple of dead idols, but the temple of the living, active, beneficent God. "What mortal man has ever heard the voice of the living God speaking out of fire, as we have, and survived?" (Deuteronomy 5:26).

Observe the richness of Paul's description of God's power and divinity: "God, the blessed and only Ruler, the King of kings and Lord of lords, who alone is immortal and who lives

in unapproachable light, whom no one has seen or can see"
(1 Timothy 6:15-16).

How easily Paul bursts into doxology! And this is one of the
finest doxologies in Scripture, each of the seven titles stressing
the incomparable greatness and transcendence of God. Let's
take a look at some of these troves.

"The blessed and only Ruler" is a phrase stressing God's relation to the universe and world rulers. He is Controller of
all things. The scope of His authority is universal—He is the
blessed and *only* Ruler, who has the right to do exactly as He
pleases. His sovereignty is inherent, not delegated. Men may
claim or be invested with honored and honorable titles, but
God alone is King over all kings and Lord over all lords. Every
other sovereignty is under His supreme control.

"Living in unapproachable light" is Paul's way of emphasiz-
ing God's inaccessibility, except as He chooses to be accessible.
God is basically beyond the scope of mere human senses. Such
are His majesty and holiness that no man could look on Him in
His unveiled glory and live. He dwells in an atmosphere so ultimately rare that mortals cannot approach Him. But although
we cannot draw very near to the sun, we can joyfully walk in
the sunshine. It is not that God is totally unapproachable, for
there is indeed a way of approach, but that path is bloodstained.

> There is a way for man to rise
> To that sublime abode,
> An offering and a sacrifice,
> A Holy Spirit's energies,
> An Advocate with God.
> —*T. Binney*

"GOD OUR SAVIOR"

The word *Savior* holds a wealth of imagery. This title is for Paul peculiar to the pastoral epistles, but the idea pervades the whole of Scripture. Paul stated, "Teach slaves . . . to show that they can be fully trusted, so that in every way they will make the teaching about God our Savior attractive" (Titus 2:9-10).

The Greek word *soter* usually means deliverer. It was used of an emperor or conqueror who delivered people from some calamity or conferred great benefits. God is truly our Savior from sin, death, and hell. He is "the Savior of all men, and especially of those who believe" (1 Timothy 4:10). Paul's statement here assures us of the *salvability* of all men, but not the *salvation* of all men. Full salvation requires the exercising of personal faith. God is in one sense the *potential* Savior because He has provided salvation for all, but He is the *actual* Savior only of those who believe.

We have a *"God who richly provides us with everything* for our enjoyment" (1 Timothy 6:17). Greek scholars point out that in this verse there is a play on words that could be rendered. "The *rich* are not to trust in uncertain *riches,* but in God, who *richly* provides everything for our enjoyment—for soul and body, for time and eternity." Ours is a beneficent and lavish God, who grants us not just a minimum of pleasure and gratification, but gives us an abundance—"everything" necessary for soul and body, for time and eternity.

Contrary to the teaching of the Gnostics of that day, to whom Paul referred in 1 Timothy 4:3, "They forbid people to marry and order them to abstain from certain foods which God created to be received with thanksgiving"—we are not only to *partake* of these things, but to *enjoy* them, with gratitude to the Giver. Only sin can prevent our enjoyment of God's lavish provision. The God of Paul, Timothy, and Titus is not only happy, sovereign, immortal, invisible, and transcendent, but also a lavish God, who gives good things in abundance.

Paul is in effect saying to young leaders everywhere, "This is the kind of God you can fully trust. You can rely on Him and even lean on Him in your service. Our God is adequate for every emergency and sufficient for every need that will arise in the ministry that lies ahead of you.

GOD THE SON

Paul's faith was centered in the person and work of Jesus Christ. To him, Christianity was Christ.

When Paul said, "To me, to live is Christ" (Philippians 1:21), he was not employing poetic license, but simply stating a literal, conscious fact. Upon his conversion and the accompanying self-surrender to his Lord, the center of life completely changed. Before then his life had been Paul but now it was Christ. Martin Luther's words in his *Table Talk* could well have been Paul's: "Should anyone knock at my heart and say 'Who lives here?' I should reply, 'Not Martin Luther, but the Lord Jesus Christ.'"

Paul's version was, "I have been crucified with Christ and I no longer live, but Christ lives in me. The life I now live in the body, I live by faith in the Son of God, who loved me and gave himself for me" (Galatians 2:20). His entire personality and all his activities were under the sway of Christ, permeated by his presence. All the ministry and sacrificial service that followed found its source in this glorious fact. Paul's life was a continuing appreciation of Christ to meet all his daily needs.

In his letter to Timothy, Paul charged him "Remember always, *as center of everything,* Jesus Christ . . . raised . . . from the dead" (2 Timothy 2:8 PH). He was not merely telling Timothy to focus his attention on the fact and doctrine of the resurrection. Rather, Paul was directing his young protégé never to forget the Person who rose from the dead, for He is in reality the center of everything. Christianity *is* Christ. From the initial moment of this revelation in Paul's mind, everything in his life revolved around Christ as center. Christ was ever on his lips and in his heart.

Paul's preaching was *Christocentric.* To the Corinthians he declared, "I resolved to know nothing while I was with you except Jesus Christ and him crucified" (1 Corinthians 2:2). Concerning his ministry in Corinth, the record of his early ministry states, "Paul devoted himself exclusively to preaching, testifying to the Jews that Jesus was the Christ" (Acts 18:5). In Thessalonica, "On three Sabbath days he reasoned with them from the Scriptures, explaining and proving that the Christ had to suffer and rise from the dead. 'This Jesus I am proclaiming to you is the Christ,' he said" (Acts 17:2-3).

These and other similar passages demonstrate how Paul accorded to Christ the central place in both life and ministry.

The Lordship of Christ was a constant emphasis of the apostle. As he used the term in his writings, the title "Lord" uniformly denoted Christ. In his initial surrender, Paul embraced without reservation Christ's lordship and absolute mastery over his life. This totality of commitment was implicit in his question, "What shall I do, *Lord?*" With quick spiritual insight, he realized that the purpose of Christ's death and resurrection went far beyond the mere salvation of the believer from judgment, having in view, moreover, the authentication of his lordship.

Paul later expressed the importance of Christ's lordship in these words: "For this very reason, Christ died and returned to life *so that he might be the Lord* of both the dead and the living" (Romans 14:9). It was the apostle's constant joy to press for recognition of "the crown rights of the Redeemer."

There is a particular phrase that appears quite often in many contexts in Paul's writings, a phrase that is especially pregnant with meaning—"in Christ." The idea behind the phrase appears to be that just as the sea is the sphere or element in which fish live, so Christians live in the sphere or element of Christ, joined to him by an invisible, yet inseparable bond. Every spiritual blessing is ours because we are *in Christ*—in a living, vital union with Him (Ephesians 1:3). A study of the occurrences of the phrase uncovers a rich vein of truth.

The greatest Christological passage in the New Testament comes from Paul's pen—Philippians 2:5-11. In this poetic confession of faith, he first affirms *the humiliation of the Son of God,* calling attention to the Son's pre-existence, incarnation, and crucifixion. Paul then unfolds *the exaltation of the Son of Man,* who shall be honored and worshiped eventually by all creation. In view of these glorious truths, the apostle exhorts, "Let this mind be in you which was also in Christ Jesus" (2:4 KJV).

GOD THE HOLY SPIRIT

Shortly before His death, in His upper room discourse, our Lord had more to say to His men about the character and ministry of the Holy Spirit than in all His previous teachings. But when speaking on that very theme, Christ made this rather mysterious statement: "I have much more to say to you, more than you can now bear. But when he, the Spirit of truth, comes, he will guide you into all truth" (John 16:12-13). It was principally through Paul that this further revelation was communicated. It is not surprising, therefore, to find his writings studded with references to the Holy Spirit, for Paul was clearly the foremost theologian of the early church.

In Paul's own experience, the Spirit played a very important part. Immediately after his conversion, Paul was filled with the Holy Spirit (Acts 9:17); so it is not surprising to find him exhorting the Ephesian Christians—and us as well—to be filled with the Spirit (Ephesians 5:18). His call to service and commissioning were through the Spirit (Acts 13:1-4). Paul was guided through both the restraint and the constraint of the Spirit (Acts 16:6-7). He depended on the Spirit's power in preaching (1 Corinthians 2:4) and the Spirit's warning when he faced impending dangers (Acts 21:4, 11-14).

Paul constantly emphasized the working of the Spirit in his preaching and teaching. As Administrator of the Church, the Spirit took the initiative in the selection of elders (Acts 20:28), and His was the authorizing voice at the first church council (Acts 15:28). When Paul met a small group of men at Ephesus, his first probing question was, "Did you receive the Holy Spirit when you believed?" (Acts 19:2), and then he guided them into that very experience.

The various names Paul used for God the Spirit bring fresh facets of the Spirit's ministry into prominence: "the Spirit of wisdom" (Ephesians 1:17), "the Spirit of holiness" (Romans

1:4), "the Spirit of sonship" (Romans 8:15), and "the Spirit of life" (Romans 8:2).

Paul taught that both justification and sanctification are the results of the Spirit's working (1 Corinthians 6:11). The Spirit inspires worship (Philippians 3:3), indwells (1 Corinthians 3:16) and strengthens us (Romans 14:17), helps in prayer (Romans 8:26-27), and dispenses joy (1 Thessalonians 1:6). The Holy Spirit is the One who promotes and maintains the unity of the church (Ephesians 4:3-4).

It was the Spirit's ministry that gave Paul victory over the *flesh*—the fallen nature that we inherited from Adam. It is only by the Spirit that we can "put to death the misdeeds of the body" (Romans 8:13). It is the Holy Spirit's delight to produce in the life of the yielded believer a cornucopia *of spiritual fruit* (Galatians 5:22-23).

Paul taught that the Holy Spirit distributes various *spiritual* gifts which are essential to the leadership, expansion, and the building up of the church. These gifts are special qualities to be desired only when they serve practical ends—the edification of the church. To be effective, every kind of ministry must be inspired and made efficient by the Holy Spirit, and these gifts are God's gracious provision to this end. Since we fight a supernatural foe, only supernatural weapons will suffice.

Two Greek words are used to describe these gifts—*pneumatikos,* things from the Spirit, and *charisma,* gifts of grace (1 Corinthians 12:1, 4). Taken together, they indicate that these extraordinary powers and endowments are sovereignly bestowed on individuals as gifts for service in the church. They are distinct from natural gifts, although they often operate through them. There is a gift for every believer (1 Corinthians

12:7), not just for some spiritual elite. These individual gifts may not be claimed as our spiritual right (1 Corinthians 12:11). To be profitable, they must be exercised in love (1 Corinthians 13:1-2). They are bestowed in order to equip us for service in the body of Christ (Ephesians 4:11-12).

No spiritual gift is to be despised, but some are more valuable than others (1 Corinthians 12:31, 14:5). Paul urges the primacy of prophecy, for the ministry of the word of God is the gift of greatest value. Leaders must beware that spiritual gifts can atrophy through neglect (1 Timothy 4:14), and thus need to be stimulated (2 Timothy 1:6).

These gifts are not given for the mere joy or aggrandizement of the beneficiary, or even for the sake of his own spiritual life, but for ministry to others (1 Corinthians 14:12), and for bringing saints to spiritual maturity (Ephesians 4:11-13). It is significant that none of the gifts refers directly to one's personal character; on the contrary, all are gifts for service.

Few people discover their gifts at the beginning of their Christian lives; thus they frequently lie dormant until the occasion reveals them. They are often more evident to others than to ourselves, but we can be sure that to the exercised heart, at the right time God will reveal the gift or combination of gifts that are necessary for fulfilling the ministry in the body of Christ that He assigns to us. In 1 Corinthians 12–14, the apostle warns the Corinthians against the unworthy use of spiritual gifts, and lays down guidelines for their exercise in the church.

Notes

1. Colquhoun, Frank, *Total Christianity* (Chicago: Moody, 1962), 60.

5

BOASTING IN THE CROSS

I resolved to know nothing while I was with you except
Jesus Christ and him crucified.

1 CORINTHIANS 2:2

In Paul's view, the Christian faith, like an ellipse, revolves around twin centers—Calvary and Pentecost, those two well-attested historical events. At his conversion, the real significance of the cross dawned on his soul, and immediately afterwards he experienced the blessings of the Holy Spirit that began at Pentecost. Henceforth his consistent attitude was expressed in the words, "May I never boast except in the cross of our Lord Jesus Christ, through which the world has been crucified to me, and I to the world" (Galatians 6:14).

The cross of Calvary was a magnificent demonstration of sacrificial love, but apart from the dynamic power released by the Holy Spirit at Pentecost, it would have been stillborn. Pentecost was the necessary complement of Calvary. The descent of the Spirit made actual in the experience of believers what Christ's death and resurrection had made possible.

Among the many facets of the death of our Lord, Paul emphasized certain relevant spiritual facts which we will deal with in this chapter.

CHRIST'S DEATH WAS A PROPITIATION FOR OUR SINS.

Paul stated that we are "justified freely by [God's] grace through the redemption that is in Christ Jesus: whom God hath set forth to be a propitiation through faith in his blood" (Romans 3:24-25 KJV). John added his witness when he said, "He is the propitiation for our sins: and not for ours only, but also for the sins of the whole world" (1 John 2:2 KJV).

This thought is absolutely basic to Christians, and bulked largely in Paul's preaching and teaching. God has declared His implacable wrath against sin, and his justice demands that all sin meet with its just retribution. Paul viewed Christ's death as a *propitiation:* a quenching of God's wrath by Christ's bearing, bearing away, and obliteration of our sins, so that they no longer stand as a barrier between us and God.

CHRIST'S DEATH PROCURED OUR DELIVERANCE FROM SIN.

Although Christ's death secured for us a full justification from all sin, giving us a righteous status before God, it would have failed in its full purpose if it had left us as victims of sin's tyranny. It is not sufficient for an external, festering sore to be superficially healed over, if the internal source of infection is not dealt with. For then its poison would continue to circulate in the bloodstream. The perfect, atoning sacrifice of our Lord does not leave us in such a tragic plight.

The purpose of Christ's death, Paul contends, is both positive and negative. "Jesus Christ . . . gave himself for us to redeem us from all wickedness and to purify for himself a people that are his very own, eager to do what is good" (Titus 2:13-14).

Our Redeemer not only bought us back but He also emancipated us from the enslavement of sin. He paid the costly ransom price in the crimson drops of His precious blood (1 Peter 1:18-19). By His victory over the devil, sin, and death, He gained for us potential deliverance from sin of every kind—*all* wickedness, whether conscious or unconscious, "respectable" or disreputable, sins of the flesh or sins of the mind.

If it is asked whether this emancipation from sin's tyranny takes place in a moment or over a period of time, the paradoxical answer is *both!* According to Paul's teaching, the crisis leading to deliverance may occur when the Christian, conscious of his inability to free himself, claims his portion of the delivering power of the cross. Then follows the process of sanctification, in which the Holy Spirit makes the potential *actual* in experience. "For we know that our old self was crucified with him so that . . . we should no longer be slaves to sin" (Romans 6:6).

Once the crisis is over, the process of sanctification accelerates and continues as long as Christ's lordship is recognized in actuality. In this process, the Holy Spirit progressively removes whatever hinders us from being transformed into the image of Christ, and leads us into the experience of Romans 6:18: "You have been set free from sin and have become slaves to righteousness."

CHRIST'S DEATH SHOULD LEAD US TO DEDICATE OURSELVES TO HIM.

The amazing grace and love that was shown on the cross demands a reciprocal response—the shifting of life's center from self to Christ. The acceptance of Christ's propitiation logically means the end of the old life or self-gratification, and the beginning of a new life centered in Him. To live for self after having taken the Lord's costly salvation is to rob Him of the fruit of his passion. "He died for all, that those who live should no longer live for themselves but for him who died for them and was raised again" (2 Corinthians 5:15).

According to Paul, a Christian's life is viewed in two dimensions—"before Christ" and "after Christ," B.C. and A.D. Until the time of conversion, the B.C. self has been the central point of reference. But after Christ enters one's life, that person's time, talents, friends, possessions, and forms of recreation are all under the Lord's control.

Contrary to worldly expectations, such an embracing of the cross of Christ, such a complete surrender to Him as Lord, brings a liberty that can be experienced in no other way. "Through Christ Jesus the law of the Spirit of life set me free from the law of sin and death" (Romans 8:2). Samuel Rutherford said, "Whoso looketh on the white side of Christ's cross, and takes it up handsomely, will find it just such a burden as wings are to a bird."

Christ's death should lead us to detach ourselves from this present world system.

Paul stated that Christ's death was not merely a noble example of heroism and an expression of love, although it was both, but that it was essentially a sacrifice for sin.

But it also had a subsidiary purpose—rescuing us from the power and corrupting influence of our world. "The Lord Jesus Christ . . . gave himself for our sins to rescue us from the present evil age" (Galatians 1:3-4).

The term *age* here refers to our sinful world from the viewpoint of time and change. It is hastening to its close and has within it nothing of inherent eternal value. Paul was merely sharing his Master's view, for Jesus said, "If the world hates you, keep in mind that it hated me first. If you belonged to the world, it would love you as its own. As it is, you do not belong to the world, but I have chosen you out of the world" (John 15:18-19).

Jesus had in view something more than physical detachment from the world, for He said to his Father, "My prayer is not that you take them out of the world but that you protect them from the evil one" (John 17:15). We are to detach ourselves morally and spiritually from the world while we are in it, but it must be done in *insulation, not isolation,* as if we were living in a holy ghetto. Believers are the salt of the earth, but salt can exercise its antiseptic and pungent influence only when there is contact. It is when we can say with Paul, "The world has been crucified to me, and I to the world" (Galatians

6:14), that we can make our greatest impact on the evil age in which we live. Compromise with the spirit of the age short-circuits the power of the eternal Spirit, and thus neutralizes our spiritual influence.

CHRIST'S DEATH WAS THE LOGICAL MEANS TO PROCURE HIS ENTHRONEMENT.

"Christ died and returned to life so that he might be the Lord of both the dead and the living" (Romans 14:9). Could words more simply and explicitly state the ultimate purpose of the cross? In the previous passages we have been considering Christ's purpose *for us* in His death. Here the focus is on the purpose of the cross *for himself*—to obtain complete sovereignty over the lives of those for whom He died, in time and in eternity.

Peter proclaimed the indisputable fact that "Jesus Christ is Lord of all" (Acts 10:36)—but this universal Lord yearns for our spontaneous recognition of that fact. Too many Christians are willing to accept all the benefits of his Saviorhood but reluctant to bow to His full sovereignty. Paul envisioned a day when recognition of Christ's sovereignty will be universal—for "at the name of Jesus every knee should bow, in heaven and on earth" (Philippians 2:10). But our Master yearns for that kind of adoration long before that day; He would far prefer a voluntary coronation, rather than a compulsory recognition.

Ideally that coronation day should take place at conversion; but if Christ's claims to lordship are not fully realized at that time, then He should be enthroned as soon as that sovereignty is recognized. William Borden, the young American

millionaire who died on his way to the mission field, described
that step of coronation:

> Lord Jesus, I take my hands off as far as my life is concerned.
> I put Thee on the throne of my heart.
> Change, cleanse me, use me as Thou shalt choose.

6

THE PRAYER WARRIOR

*Paul was a leader by appointment and by universal recognition
and acceptance. He had many mighty forces in this ministry. His
conversion, so conspicuous and radical, was a great force, a perfect
magazine of aggressive and defensive warfare. His call to the
apostleship was clear, luminous and convincing. But these forces were
not the divinest energies which brought forth the largest results to
his ministry. Paul's course was more distinctly shaped and his career
rendered more powerfully successful by prayer than by any other force.*

E. M. BOUNDS

To read Paul's letters is to discover the supremely important place of prayer in the life of a spiritual leader. Nowhere does a leader expose the quality of his own spiritual life more clearly than in his prayers. We should be deeply grateful, therefore, for the unstudied self-revelation in the prayers that abound in the apostle's letters. He is at his best in his prayers.

It is obvious that Paul did not regard prayer as supplemental, but as fundamental—not something to be added to his work but the very matrix out of which his work was born. He was a man of action *because* he was a man of prayer. It was probably his prayer even more than his preaching that produced the kind of leaders we meet in his letters.

It is significant that nowhere does Paul argue the reasonableness or possibility of prayer. He does not even make an attempt to explain it, but assumes it to be the natural and normal expression of the spiritual life. Paul did not seem to fret over failure to meet his prayer obligations as we often do, and he never seemed to be plagued with the condemning heart that robbed him of his confidence. He considered nothing to be beyond the reach of prayer.

> Prayer is the Christian's vital breath,
> The Christian's native air,
> His watchword at the gate of death,
> He enters heaven with prayer.
>
> —J. Montgomery
> The Elements of True Prayer

Paul's recorded prayers do not seem to be formal or highly structured, and yet they are anything but slovenly or haphazard. It is clear that they did not just happen, but that they were the outcome of careful thought. A study of Paul's prayers reveals a depth of adoration, a height of thanksgiving, and a breadth of intercession that leaves one in awe.

At times the apostle breaks out into doxology, his whole soul flaming up to heaven like incense on the altar fire. At other times his prayer is quiet and contemplative. An old divine asserted that our prayers are often cold, dry, and repetitious because there is so little of Christ in them. But no such charge could be made against Paul. As we stand at his prison door and listen to the prayers that ascended there, we are reminded of his Master's prayer recorded in John 17.

While it is true that prayer should not be clinically analyzed, there is a sense in which it can be legitimately divided into its constituent elements. A study of Paul's prayers reveals a remarkable balance. The elements that go into making up a balanced prayer life are easily discernible. *Worship and adoration* are prominent dimensions of prayer—prostrating the soul before God in contemplation—paying Him the reverence and honor that are His due. In his worship, Paul ascribed praise for what God *is,* as well as for what He *does.*

Paul's prayers were replete with *thanksgiving and praise*— the appreciative acknowledgment of the benefits and blessings God gives, whether to ourselves or to others.

Confession of sin had no rightful place in the life of our Lord, but this was not so in the case of the apostle. In his letters and addresses, he expressed an acute sense of his own sin. "I know that nothing good lives in me, that is, in my sinful nature. For I have the desire to do what is good, but I cannot carry it out . . . . The evil I do not want to do—this I keep on doing" (Romans 7:18-19).

> Oh the regret, the struggle and the failing!
> Oh the days desolate and useless years!
> Vows in the night, so fierce and unavailing!
> Sting of my shame and passion of my tears.
> —F. W. H Myers

The next major element in prayer is *petition*—bringing your daily and recurring needs before your heavenly Father, who "knows what you need before you ask him" (Matthew 6:8). It is striking to note the priorities in prayer established by our Lord in His well-known exemplary prayer (Matthew 6:9-13). Not until halfway through the prayer is there any mention of personal needs. The first part is taken up with God and our relations with Him.

A similarly proportioned emphasis can be discerned in Paul's prayers. He was not an ascetic who had no needs, and yet his needs did not come first in his order of priorities. Most of his prayers were concerned with the needs of others. But he did not neglect to bring his own daily needs, both temporal and spiritual, before the Lord in confident expectation of their satisfaction.

A great portion of Paul's prayers dealt with *intercession*—the presentation of the personal needs of others at the throne of grace. This is the unselfish side of prayer. Paul was constantly praying for his converts and churches.

Intercession does not have in view the overcoming of the reluctance of God, but the claiming of the merits of Christ on behalf of others who are in a bad situation. The spiritual development of his flock was the lifeblood of Paul's experience, as we see in his prayers of intercession.

> Others, dear Lord, Yes, others,
> This all my prayer shall be;
> Help me to live for others,
> That I may live like Thee.

It was the experience of Henry Martyn that during times of spiritual dryness and depression—and who doesn't have such experiences?—he often found "a delightful revival in the act of praying for others, for their conversion or sanctification, or prosperity in the work of the Lord."[1]

THE CHARACTERISTICS OF TRUE PRAYER

Referring to men who had led the vanguard in evangelistic and revival work E. M. Bounds said, "They were not leaders because of brilliancy of thought, because they were exhaustless in resources, because of their magnificent culture or native endowment, but *because of the power of prayer they could command the power of God.*"

Here we have in a nutshell the foremost secret of Paul's amazing leadership. Although he possessed many great personal qualities in rich measure, he renounced dependence on them, instead of using *prayer* as his primary channel for the implementation of divine power.

Paul's prayers serve as a model for leaders who carry spiritual responsibility. Consider the element of perseverance in his prayers. They were *unceasing.* "Night and day I constantly remember you in my prayers" (2 Timothy 1:3).

This does not mean that Paul did nothing else. He used the word *unceasing* in the sense of "incessant," or "ever recurring." An incessant cough is not one that never stops, but one that constantly persists. When Paul's mind was free of other concerns, be it day or night, his heart turned to prayer, as the needle to the magnetic pole.

In other words, Paul was not using the language of

exaggeration. Perhaps we find such constancy difficult to envision because our minds are so secularized—engrossed with things on a level separate from God. But to the apostolic prayer warrior, *everything* was a cause for prayer or praise to God.

For Paul praying was a *strenuous* endeavor. "I want you to know how much I am struggling for you and for those at Laodicea" (Colossians 2:1). This is an aspect of praying that many people seldom experience. Prayer should not be a comfortable, dreamy reverie. There is certainly a restful aspect of prayer, but it should not be an escape from reality or a vacation from responsibility. "Prayer is never meant to be *indolently easy*, however simple and reliant it may be." said Bishop Moule.

Prayer regarded as conflict or struggle includes the ideas of toil and strife. Paul knew that true prayer arouses mighty position in the unseen realm. There is a Greek word sometimes translated *struggle* in the phrase, "the good *fight* of the faith" (1 Timothy 6:12). This is a vivid and strong word concept, from which we derive our word *agonize*. Paul uses it elsewhere when describing an *athlete* competing in the arena (1 Corinthians 9:25), a *soldier* battling for his life (1 Timothy 6:12), and a *laborer* toiling until he is weary (Colossians 1:29). How pallid and tepid do our prayers appear in comparison! Paul's prayers often built up to the crescendo of a spiritual groaning (2 Corinthians 5:2-4). The apostle was indeed a tenacious prayer warrior.

> How have I knelt with arms of my aspiring
> Lifted all night in irresponsive air,
> Dazed and amazed with overmuch desiring
> Blank with the utter agony of prayer.

Shame on the flame so dying to an ember!
Shame on the reed so lightly overset!
Yes, I have seen Him, can I not remember?
Yes, I have known Him, and shall Paul forget?
                                    —*F. W. H. Myers*

Paul infused a very *submissive* dimension in his prayers. For once he had discovered the will of God, he was content with it. There are some who contend that the phrase "if it be Your will" in a prayer is negation of faith. Although this may sometimes be true, it is not necessarily true in all cases. Jesus prayed, "My Father, if it is not possible for this cup to be taken away unless I drink it, may your will be done" (Matthew 26:42). Paul believed in a wisdom and a will beyond his own. And when the Father's will became plain, he cordially accepted a divine refusal, and counted on the sufficiency of divine grace to enable him to triumph.

"Three times I pleaded with the Lord to take [the thorn] away from me. But he said to me 'My grace is sufficient for you, for my power is made perfect in weakness.' Therefore I will boast all the *more gladly* about my weaknesses, so that Christ's power may rest on me" (2 Corinthians 12:8-9).

Paul's prayers were *confident.* The seeming impossibility of a situation did not daunt him or discourage the importance of prayer. To a man who constantly lived in the realm of the supernatural and held constant converse with the omnipotent God, nothing was impossible except that which was beyond the scope of the divine will. When Paul prayed, he confidently expected the supernatural intervention of God, if indeed it was necessary. He knew no circumstances in which prayer was not appropriate.

A typical example of this confidence is recorded in Acts 27:23-26. "Last night," Paul reported, "an angel of the God whose I am and whom I serve stood beside me and said, 'Do not be afraid, Paul. You must stand trial before Caesar; and God has graciously given you the lives of all who sail with you.' So keep up your courage, men, for I have faith in God that it will happen just as he told me."

The apostle Paul's prayers were *covetous*. We can find encouragement in the fact that even the great apostle, one of the greatest exponents of the art of prayer, was not self-sufficient. He was often made conscious of his inadequacy in many areas, and felt a strong need for the Holy Spirit's help. "The Spirit helps us in our weakness. *We do not know what we ought to pray,* but the Spirit himself intercedes for us with groans that words cannot express" (Romans 8:26).

Paul coveted the prayers of his fellow believers. Indeed he regarded their prayers for himself not as a desirable addendum, but as an important determining factor in his ministry. His letters contain many pleas for prayer fellowship. Paul wrote to his spiritual family in Philippi, "I know that through your prayers and the help given by the Spirit of Jesus Christ, what has happened to me will turn out for my deliverance" (Philippians 1:19). Paul and his converts engaged in a mutual prayer life.

Thus we see that Paul regarded prayer as *a cooperative effort* within the church. "Brothers, pray for us," he asked the newly converted Thessalonian believers (1 Thessalonians 5:25). To the Corinthians he wrote, "On [God] we have set our hope that he will continue to deliver us, as you help us by your prayers" (2 Corinthians 1:10-11).

Paul craved the prayers of others for such matters as being able to speak boldly. "Pray also for me, that whenever I open my mouth, words may be given me" (Ephesians 6:19). Paul asked God not only to open his mouth, but also to open doors of opportunity. "Pray for us, too, that God may open a door for our message" (Colossians 4:3).

Paul's prayers always seemed to be *strategic*. There were no trivialities in them. He prayed for things central to the divine purpose and to the growth and maturity of the church. His prayers reveal the factors which he deemed of paramount importance.

In the prayer of Colossians 2:1-3, Paul epitomized some of the greatest needs of young converts and emerging churches. For here he was praying for people he had never seen, a fact which should encourage us in praying for missionary situations. He prayed for their *encouragement* in the face of strong temptation toward discouragement—"that they may be encouraged in heart." He likewise prayed for their *unity*. In the midst of satanic attempts to promote division, he prayed "that they may be . . . united in love."

Paul prayed furthermore for their *assurance*—"so that they may have the full riches of complete understanding." And finally, he prayed for their *knowledge* of "the mystery of God, namely, Christ." This powerful prayer forms a practical model for all Christian leaders.

Paul's prayers were always *Spirit-inspired*. He counted on the Holy Spirit to complement his weakness and inadequacy (Romans 8:26-27). And it is indeed the Spirit's delight to come to the aid of spiritual leaders in their weaknesses.

We all labor under a threefold handicap, and the Spirit aids us in each area: (1) Despite *the iniquity of our hearts,* which tends to discourage prayer and bring condemnation, the Spirit leads us to the cleansing power of the blood of Christ, that mighty solvent for all sin. (2) *The ignorance of our minds is* easily overcome by the Spirit, who knows the mind and will of God and communicates it freely to the obedient and receptive heart. The Spirit lets us know whether the content of our prayer is or is not the will of God. (3) *The weakness of our bodies* often acts as a blockade to prayer. The Spirit helps us to rise above adverse physical conditions of either health or climate.

In the area of prayer, it is important to be alert so that we do not slip into unconscious and unintentional independence of the Holy Spirit. For we are always to "pray in the Spirit," as Paul exhorts us in Ephesians 6:18: "Pray in the Spirit on all occasions with all kinds of prayers and requests."

Notes

1. Moule, Handley C. G., *Secret Prayer* (London: Marshall's), 113.

7

A COMMUNICATOR FOR GOD

Since, then, we know what it is to fear the Lord,
we try to persuade men.

2 CORINTHIANS 5:11

Without doubt one of the most potent elements in Paul's leadership was his ability to communicate divine truth powerfully and convincingly. Most truly effective leaders possess this ability.

In World War II, Adolph Hitler and Winston Churchill were the outstanding figures. Hitler's pronouncements were not usually worthy of note, but he spoke wisely when he claimed, "The power which has set in motion the greatest avalanches of power in politics and religion has been from the beginning of time the magic of the spoken word."[1] His own frenzied speeches vindicated his viewpoint.

Winston Churchill in like manner led and galvanized the free world into action as much by his measured, intrepid, inspiring speeches at critical moments as by his great political and military gifts.

In modern parlance, Paul would be described as a superb communicator. He was essentially a preacher, a flaming herald of the good news. If the success of preaching is gauged by the results it achieves, then Paul was a preacher *par excellence*. He earned the right to exhort Timothy, "Preach the Word; be prepared in season and out of season" (2 Timothy 4:2).

The humble apostle laid no claim to a superior oratorical gift. "When I came to you, brothers, I did not come with eloquence or superior wisdom as I proclaimed to you the testimony about God" (1 Corinthians 2:1). His reliance was on the Holy Spirit, not on worldly sophistry. "My message and my preaching were not with wise and persuasive words, but with a demonstration of the Spirit's power" (1 Corinthians 2:4).

A Dynamic Method of Communication

In keeping with the flexibility of his mind, Paul's method of communication was adapted to the occasion. At times it was *polemical*. He satisfied his hearers' reasoning by presenting incontrovertible proofs. "Saul grew more and more powerful and baffled the Jews living in Damascus by proving that Jesus is the Christ" (Acts 9:22). He did not adopt evasive tactics when confronted with a difficult argument, nor was he an intellectual coward, afraid to accept a challenge in defense of his beliefs. His pulpit was no coward's castle.

Paul's presentation of truth was carefully reasoned. "He reasoned in the synagogue with the Jews and the God-fearing Greeks, as well as in the marketplace day by day with those who happened to be there" (Acts 17:17). His objective was not merely to win the argument, but to win his opponents for Christ.

Paul's method of communication was *persuasive*. He did not simply present cold facts with convincing logic and leave it there, but he accompanied his appeal with warm entreaty. He preferred to convince rather than to command or warn. "Every Sabbath he reasoned in the synagogue, trying to persuade Jews and Greeks" (Acts 18:4).

Paul believed in a coming judgment—that God was not an indulgent spiritual grandfather, but a God of judgment who hates sin with an implacable hatred and who will eventually purge it from the universe. This belief lent urgency to Paul's pleadings. "Since, then, we know what it is to fear the Lord, we try to persuade men" (2 Corinthians 5:11). And in this art of persuasion, he was singularly successful. "Paul entered the synagogue and spoke boldly there for three months, arguing persuasively about the kingdom of God" (Acts 19:8).

> Oh could I tell, ye surely would believe it!
>   Oh could I only say what I have seen!
> How should I tell, or how could you receive it,
>   How till He bringeth you where I have been?
>
> Give me a voice, a cry and a complaining—
>   Oh let my sound be stormy in their ears!
> Throat that would shout, but cannot stay for straining,
>   Eyes that would weep, but cannot wait for tears.
>   —*F. W. H. Myers*

The preaching of the apostle was often *didactic*—adapted in order to meet the special needs of his hearers. For Paul was both preacher and teacher. Two major periods of extended preaching and teaching are recorded: two years in the school of Tyrannus, and eighteen months in Corinth (Acts 19:9-10, 18:11). He frequently adopted the method of question and answer to clinch his teaching. Since people must have a factual basis for an intelligent faith, he painstakingly instructed them in the concrete operations of God.

Although Paul's teaching method was very solid, it was also commendably *versatile*. There was nothing stereotyped in his approach. He suited his message to his audience, as we see in his address at Athens. While the basic content of his message remained constant, he realized the importance of establishing common ground with those he addressed, whether Jewish congregations in the synagogues, Greek philosophers at the Acropolis, or pagan crowds at Lystra. He was equally at home with governors and officials, philosophers, theologians, and workingmen.

As to the tone of his preaching, Paul could not be charged with "the curse of a dry-eyed Christianity." "Remember," he exhorted the Ephesians, "that for three years I never stopped warning each of you night and day with tears" (Acts 20:31). And again the apostle spoke of his weeping: "As I have often told you before and now say again even with tears, many live as enemies of the cross of Christ" (Philippians 3:18). There is something moving in manly tears. But Paul was not ashamed of his tears for the cause of Christ.

Mars Hill: Failure or Success?

Paul's address in Athens on Mars Hill, recorded in Acts 17:22-31, is regarded by some as his greatest failure in communication. Their interpretation is that, instead of preaching "Christ and him crucified," he pandered to the distinguished, erudite philosophers, thus bungling his opportunity. In support of their position, they quote his affirmation to the Corinthians, "I resolved to know nothing while I was with you except Jesus Christ and him crucified" (1 Corinthians 2:2), interpreting this as a reflection of Paul's determination to change his approach.

Others, however, view Paul's Athenian address as one of his greatest messages, and allege that his approach could not be improved on. S. M. Zwemer called it "a marvel of tactful and powerful preaching." F. B. Myer said, "For its grace and intellectual sequence, grandeur of conception and range, stately march of eloquent words, it stands alone."[2] Paul was probably disappointed at the reception accorded his message by the majority; but was it Paul who failed, or the Athenians?

Whichever view is taken, this address gives helpful insight into Paul's communication techniques. In it he displayed his amazing versatility in becoming "all things to all men"—an intellectual to the intellectuals of Athens—"so that by all possible means" he might save some (1 Corinthians 9:22). In this he was extremely successful.

Let us analyze the results of his preaching at Athens (Acts 17:32-34), which even Alexander Maclaren dismissed as "little less than naught."

Some *sneered.* Some of the people present took part in ironical mocking, or cynical disdain of Paul's message.

Some *temporized.* They said, "We want to hear you again on this subject" (17:31), but they procrastinated in indecision.

Some *believed.* "A few men became followers of Paul and

believed" (17:34). Thus some of the people present embraced Paul's message. "Among them was Dionysius, a member of the Areopagus" (17:34).

The Areopagus was the high court of twelve judges in Athens. A modern equivalent of the believing of Dionysius would be the conversion of a justice of the United States Supreme Court. If such a conversion were to take place because of the message of some contemporary preacher, would that address be considered a failure? How often are leading jurists converted? Paul himself said that not many wise people are chosen by God (1 Corinthians 1:26). Sources from tradition tell us that this same Dionysius later became Bishop of Corinth.

Another convert was Damaris, a foreign and well-educated aristocratic woman. It has been suggested that she was probably a "God-fearer" who had previously heard Paul preach in the synagogue. "And a number of others" also believed. Not a bad catch for one address to a group of mentally sated intellectuals! Many preachers today would be happy to experience such a failure!

One point to be borne in mind in assessing Paul's message is that it was interrupted and cut short, with no opportunity for him to complete it; thus we have no idea of its full content. Furthermore, there is no need for us to conclude that the greatly condensed report in Acts 17 comprises all that he said. For the content of his message seems to be summarized here in Scripture, as we see in verse 18: "They said this because Paul was preaching the good news about Jesus and the resurrection."

There is much for the Christian leader to learn from Paul's approach. We can see that he constantly adapted himself to his audience. In addressing the people of Pisidian Antioch, he appealed almost entirely to the Old Testament Scriptures with which they were familiar (Acts 13:14-41).

In speaking to the peasants at Lystra, however, Paul expressed similar thoughts in different language. He used no Old Testament references, for they were ignorant of them, but appealed instead to the beneficence of God (Acts 14:15-18).

At Athens, in addressing Greek philosophers Paul established rapport by quoting their own poets, and gave a biblical philosophy of their history, following up with a reasoned discourse about the nature of the Godhead.

Paul's flexibility of mind in thus adapting his message to his audience illustrates his phrase, becoming "all things to all men." The lesson for the missionary is that he should study the literature and culture of the people so that he will be able to speak on their wavelength, especially to the leaders or potential leaders of the group.

Paul's conciliatory prelude to his Athenian address is a model for emulation. With great tact and courtesy, he introduced his subject by complimenting the people on their obvious religious interest manifested in the many altars around the city. He did not begin by combating their idols. That would come later, after rapport had been established. Nor did he quote Jewish references, with which they would be unfamiliar.

Although Paul was quite flexible, he was not compromising. The apostle did not come down to the level of his philosophy-oriented hearers, as though Christianity were just another philosophy. Instead, he endeavored to find a point in their current beliefs to which he could attach his own message. Because he was out to win them rather than an intellectual argument, he limited himself to a comment on one particular inscription upon an altar which had caught his eye. He had his point of contact: "TO AN UNKNOWN GOD." With seeming audacity Paul said, "Now what you worship as something unknown I am going to proclaim to you" (Acts 17:23).

Paul first emphasized points of similarity rather than points of difference in order to gain their attention to his message. But after achieving this end, he launched into a polemic against idolatry. His courtesy did not lead him to condone error.

Dr. S. M. Zwemer points out that although it is true that Paul gave recognition to some of the positive elements he could find in Athens, he did not pander to their Attic pride, but instead he laid the ax to it. He challenged them on five major points.

(1) Although they declared themselves to have sprung from the soil, Paul asserted that *God* made the world and all things (17:24).

(2) Although they pointed proudly to the Acropolis and its beautiful architecture, Paul said, "The God who made the world and everything in it . . . does not live in temples built by hands" (17:24).

(3) Although they felt infinitely superior to the barbarians, Paul asserted, "From one man [God] made every nation of men, that they should inhabit the whole earth" (17:26).

(4) Although they prided themselves on their chronology and antiquity, Paul contended that it was *God*, not Herodotus, who

"determined the times set for them and the exact places where they should live" (17:26).

(5) Although they prided themselves in their history—the vaunted "Golden Age of Pericles"—Paul stated that this period of "such ignorance" God had graciously overlooked (17:30).

Thus did Paul rout the exclusive, pantheistic, materialistic Greeks, challenging them to repent. "The whole address remains a model for those who seek in such circles to present the Christian way of faith, and a warning to those who, in misguided moments, have seen a virtue in crudity, and a loyalty to truth in a disrespect for the views, the habits of thought, the attitudes of intelligent people who fail in all points to follow them."[3]

The apostle Paul never seemed to confine himself to preaching rigid, formal sermons. In his contact with men and women of all classes, he led up to the theme of themes in the language and cultural context of the people he was addressing.

Notes

1. Gangel, Kenneth, *So You Want to Be a Leader* (Harrisburg: Christian Publications, 1973), 14.

2. Meyer, F. B., *Paul,* 122.

3. Blaiklock, Edward M., *Bible Characters* (London: Scripture Union, 1974), 127.

8

THE TRAILBLAZING
MISSIONARY

*Our hope is that, as your faith continues to grow, our area of
activity among you will greatly expand so that we can preach
the gospel in the regions beyond you.*

2 CORINTHIANS 10:15-16

The apostle Paul was a missionary trailblazer, leaving
behind him a string of new churches pulsating with
life. It is a significant fact that the greatest missionary
advances of this century have followed the rediscovery or re-
emphasis of Paul's missionary principles.

Writing of Paul in his role as a missionary prototype, Dr.
R. E. Speer, himself a notable missionary statesman, said, "The
first missionary marked out for all time the lines and principles of successful missionary work."

It is usually thought that Paul's Damascus road experience
was the root cause of his missionary enthusiasm, and in a
sense this is true. But was he not already an ardent missionary

for Judaism before his conversion? He wanted to be a missionary as well as a rabbi. Was this not at the root of the man's excessive persecuting zeal? Far from quenching this missionary passion, his conversion only intensified it, but radically oriented its direction.

By teaching and example, Paul approximated the divine pattern more nearly than any other missionary the world has seen. In him, Christ possessed an instrument uniquely qualified, finely tuned, and passionately devoted to the divine purpose. Indeed, Christ chose him precisely because he saw in him missionary raw material of unusual quality. Other missionaries, such as David Livingstone, have opened continents to the gospel. Paul opened a world.

His general calling from the Lord has been treated earlier, but we need to consider it further in relation to his subsequent missionary activities. On the Damascus road, the Lord intimated two unique things to Paul concerning his missionary service: (1) his ministry would be to distant lands; (2) it would be primarily to Gentiles (Acts 22:21). Since Jesus was sent first and foremost to "the lost sheep of the house of Israel" (Matthew 10:6 KJV), he had to leave the evangelization of the Gentiles to his followers, of whom Paul was to be the leader.

The universal character of the gospel was apprehended by the apostles only slowly. A significant step in this direction was made when Peter overcame his narrow bigotry, going to the house of Cornelius, a Roman centurion (Acts 10:9-48). But subsequent events in Galatia proved that his prejudice had not been entirely dispelled (Galatians 2:11-14). The conversion of the Gentiles on a world scale demanded someone with a broader mind and a larger heart than Peter's. In Paul the Holy

Spirit found a big-hearted, uniquely prepared instrument. But it was only through a gradual process that Paul understood all the implications of his call (Acts 13:46; 18:6; 22:19-21).

It has been rightly contended that the call of the missionary today is not some new purpose of God for his life, but the discovery of the purpose for which God sent him into the world—the culmination of a divine preparation that began before his birth. It was so with Paul. His career as a missionary was one of steady expansion. As he went forward in obedience, the plan of God for his life gradually began to take shape. His career was a demonstration of the fact that the blessing of God rests in unusual measure on the frontiers of missionary advance.

METHODS OF MISSIONARY LEADERSHIP

The book of Acts was the world's first missionary manual embodying both the history and the philosophy of mission. It abounds in typical missionary scenes and events which afford valuable guidance for mission in every age. It reports failures as well as successes. It uncovers principles and indicates methods. Acts is God's commentary on problems encountered on most mission fields today. Covering as it does a period of thirty-three years, it is a graphic demonstration of what can be accomplished in a lifetime by ordinary men and women who simply obey God.

In considering the methods Paul employed as the human leader of the missionary enterprise of the early church, we note several points:

(1) As he planned his strategy, Paul "recognized that missions was a human task involving man in his total relationships and in his national, social and cultural identity. Thus *he sought to identify himself* as nearly as possible *with the national and social strata of mankind* in order to present the gospel intelligibly and acceptably" (1 Corinthians 9:16-23).[1] He accordingly adapted his tactics to his strategy.

(2) He *did not confine his endeavors to any one stratum of society.* In this sense Paul was willing to become "all things to all men." He aimed to reach both the underprivileged and the influential. "I am obligated both to Greeks and non-Greeks, both to the wise and the foolish. That is why I am so eager to preach the gospel also to you who are at Rome" (Romans 1:14-15).

(3) *He bypassed villages and small towns in order to concentrate on the more strategic large cities,* since they exercise more influence on the culture and habits of the people. Only in this way could consistent growth be ensured.

(4) *Paul regarded every home church and its individual members as a potential sending base.* He expected them to function as such in a comparatively short time. The Thessalonian church brought much joy to him in this regard. "You became a model to all the believers in Macedonia and Achaia. The Lord's message rang out from you not only in Macedonia and Achaia—your faith in God has become known everywhere" (1 Thessalonians 1:7-8).

(5) *He pursued a policy of steady expansion, but did not neglect a ministry of consolidation in places already visited* (Romans 15:20). "Let us go back and visit the brothers in all the towns where we preached the word of the Lord and see how they are doing" (Acts 15:36). Letters were part of his pastoral care of the churches.

(6) *Paul engaged in consistent and persistent itineration and personal evangelism.* He did not make the mistake of some leaders who counsel others to do what they themselves fail to do.

(7) *He championed the cause of the Gentiles against the legalists,* preaching that all barriers have been done away with in Christ. "There is neither Jew nor Greek, slave nor free, male nor female, for you are all one in Christ Jesus" (Galatians 3:28). Distinctions of race, class, and sex were out.

(8) *Paul renounced superficial methods of evangelism.* Mere evangelism did not satisfy him. Paul's objective was to plant permanent churches among people responsive to the truth, and to lead believers into full maturity. He stated the aim of his preaching succinctly in Colossians 1:28-29: "We proclaim him, admonishing and teaching everyone with all wisdom, so that we may present everyone perfect in Christ. To this end I labor, struggling with all his energy, which so powerfully works in me."

When converts were won, Paul formed them into churches with a simple and flexible organization. He "preached the good news . . . and won a large number of disciples . . . Paul and

Barnabas appointed elders for them in each church and, with prayer and fasting, committed them to the Lord in whom they had put their trust" (Acts 14:21, 23).

(9) *He preached a complete gospel*—the universality of sin and the certainty of judgment, the importance and sufficiency of the cross, and the resurrection and second coming of Christ. "I declared to you today that I am innocent of the blood of all men. For I have not hesitated to proclaim to you the whole will of God" (Acts 20:26-27). Even when in Thessalonica for only a short time, Paul presented the whole range of truth in embryonic form.

(10) *He offered no financial baits,* but on the contrary encouraged each church to be not only self-supporting, but also generous in giving to others. When writing to the Corinthians, Paul cited the example of the Macedonian church which gave "even beyond their ability" (2 Corinthians 8:3). He encouraged them by saying, "Just as you excel in everything—in faith, in speech, in knowledge, in complete earnestness and in your love for us—see that you also excel in this grace of giving (8:7).

(11) *Paul practiced the art of delegation.* Although he was willing to carry a tremendous load of work and responsibility himself, he was wise enough not to assume too much responsibility for the churches. He knew how to delegate responsibility to others who, though perhaps less qualified, would grow and develop as they were entrusted with more responsibility. He thus kept on developing new leadership.

(12) In saying, "Follow my example, as I follow the example of Christ" (1 Corinthians 11:1), Paul was setting a tremendously high standard, especially in the area of sacrificial service. *He set for his converts a standard no lower than he himself demonstrated.*

(13) *Paul searched out and cultivated the friendship of promising young men with leadership potential,* schooling them to discipline themselves as good soldiers for Jesus Christ. "Train yourself to be godly," he urged Timothy. "For physical training is of some value, but godliness has value for all things, holding promise for both the present life and the life to come" (1 Timothy 4:7-8).

(14) Whenever it was the wisest course under the circumstances, *he took no support* from the churches, but earned his living at tentmaking.

(15) *He had unbounded confidence in the message of the gospel,* and in its power to transform individuals and communities (Romans 1:15-17).

(16) *He had the spirit of the spiritual pioneer.* "Our hope is that, as your faith continues to grow, our area of activity among you will greatly expand, so that we can preach the gospel in the regions beyond you. For we do not want to boast about work already done in another man's territory" (2 Corinthians 10:15-16).

To Paul, closed doors were not so much an obstacle as a challenge. He did not assume that just because a door seemed to be closed he should not attempt to enter in. Nor did he stand idly by and allow the devil to have an uncontested victory. He pushed the door to see if it would swing open (Acts 16:7), but accepted God's will without any objections when it became clear—even when it went contrary to his desires.

Sometimes duty hindered the apostle from fulfilling his objective. "I planned many times to come to you (but have been prevented from doing so until now)" (Romans 1:13). Sometimes it was Satan who hindered him. "We wanted to come to you—certainly I, Paul did, again and again—but Satan stopped us" (1 Thessalonians 2:18). But usually Paul was successful in achieving his objective.

What a man! What a missionary! He richly earned Dean Farrar's assessment of him and his qualities: "Paul, energetic as Peter and contemplative as John; Paul, the hero of unselfishness; Paul, the mighty champion of religious liberty; Paul, a greater preacher than Chrysostom, a greater missionary than Xavier, a greater reformer than Luther, a greater theologian than St. Thomas Aquinas; Paul, the inspired apostle of the Gentiles, the slave of the Lord Jesus Christ."[2]

THE DISAGREEMENT WITH BARNABAS

Missionaries are not exempt from the attacks of the adversary, who is always on the alert to disturb harmony. Even godly men have their Achilles heel, and Paul was no exception. The disagreement between him and Barnabas over John Mark holds salutary lessons for the missionary leader.

On Paul's first missionary tour, John Mark defected and returned home from Perga. In Paul's eyes this was a serious dereliction of duty. When Barnabas wished to take John Mark with them on their second tour, Paul strongly objected. He considered the young man to have neither the spirit nor the stamina for such a hazardous journey.

It was not mild disagreement that resulted. "They had such a sharp disagreement that they parted company," runs the record (Acts 15:36-39). Barnabas's action smacked of nepotism, for John Mark was his nephew. He was caught in a clash of loyalties, and opted in favor of his relative. In the heat of the argument, he became obstinate and Paul was intransigent. They reached an impasse, and there is no record that they prayed together about it. Instead, they reached the unhappy solution of going different ways.

In retrospect it seems that there were elements of right in both viewpoints. Barnabas felt that the young man should be given the benefit of a second chance, and that he would ultimately make good. He proved to be right. Paul thought more of the importance of achieving their task; thus he felt it was an unwarranted risk to take a team member who would be likely to defect again when the going got difficult. His reasoning is not difficult to follow.

Sir William Ramsay maintains that history marches with Paul, not Barnabas, for he was the one who received the blessing of the Antioch church. On the other hand, Barnabas's optimistic conviction of the salvability of the young man proved well-founded, and so Paul later wrote to Timothy, "Get Mark and bring him with you, because he is helpful to me in my ministry" (2 Timothy 4:11). This was the mark of a big man, a true leader.

Apparently the lesson to Mark proved salutary as well,

opening his eyes to his own character defect. This personal insight doubtless threw him back on God's help.

The quarrel between Paul and Barnabas cannot be justified or condoned, but God "turned the curse into a blessing" (Deuteronomy 23:5). The end result was the creation of two effective preaching teams. The quarrel was no fruit of the Spirit, but, once again, "Where sin increased, grace increased all the more" (Romans 5:20).

Such a situation is an ever-present possibility in Christian work—differences of opinion issuing in prayerless argument that results in a breach of fellowship. "These things . . . were written for our instruction (1 Corinthians 10:11 NASB).

Notes

1. Peters, George W., *Biblical Theology of Missions* (Chicago: Moody, 1972), 165.

2. Sanders, *Bible Men of Faith,* 219.

9

THE VIEWS OF A COMMITTED MAN

It is written, "I believed; therefore I have spoken." With that same
spirit of faith we also believe and therefore speak.

2 CORINTHIANS 4:13

An open mind and a tolerant attitude are highly extolled in intellectual circles, and rightly so, provided the terms of reference are right. But there is an openness of mind and tolerance that is simply spinelessness.

On many subjects it is quite right to suspend judgment—matters that are morally neutral, speculative interpretations of Scripture on which there is no clear word, or other issues on which alternative views are justified.

But there are some matters on which it is right to have a closed mind. When a Christian, after thorough thought and scriptural research, has arrived at settled conclusions, he is right to maintain his convictions. "Each one should be fully convinced in his own mind" (Romans 14:5).

Does a student of mathematics have an open mind concerning whether two plus two equals four? No. But this does not mean that one must not be ready to consider other seemingly indisputable facts. Such an evasion would merit the charge of obscurantism. But one should indeed require incontrovertible evidence to make him change his mind. In the Christian life, we must work our way toward settled convictions as our anchorage in the restless sea of life.

A conviction is "a strong belief on the ground of satisfactory evidence, without any implication of previous error" (Webster). Opinions cost us only breath, but convictions often cost life itself. We are all prolific in opinions, but few fight their way through to strong convictions. Some people confuse prejudices with convictions, but prejudice only makes us bigots. We must arrive at certitude on the basic facts of our faith.

Like every strong leader, Paul cherished strong convictions—convictions that were like steel, strong and durable. He had unshakable beliefs concerning God and man, life and death, this world and the next. These beliefs lent color and authority to his leadership. People love to follow a person who truly believes his beliefs. As A. T. Robertson wrote in *The Glory of the Ministry*: "It is not a preacher's wisdom but his conviction which imparts itself to others. Real flame kindles another flame. Men with convictions will speak and will be heard . . . . No amount of reading or intellectual brilliance will take the place of thorough conviction and sincerity."[1]

Convictions are not the product of reason and research alone. There is something more that propels the believers forward to commitment.

The heart has reasons that reason does not know. It is the heart that feels God, not the reason. There are truths that are felt and truths that are proved, for we know the truth not only by reason but by the intuitive conviction which may be called the heart. The primary truths are not demonstrable and *yet* our knowledge of them is nonetheless certain . . . . Truth may be above reason and yet not contrary to reason.[2]

The apostle Paul held firm viewpoints on issues confronting him as a leader in the church. In this chapter, we shall examine many of his deep convictions.

THE NATURE OF SCRIPTURE

The convictions of a leader concerning the Bible will affect profoundly the nature of his leadership. One who has mental reservations about the absolute inspiration and authority of Scripture will inevitably have only a tentative note in his handling and application of divine truth. Here, as elsewhere, Paul sets the standard. His mind was tuned to the mind of God.

Paul's only Bible was the Old Testament, and even before his conversion he treated it with reverence as the oracles of God. In his training he would commit large tracts of it to memory, an invaluable practice too little observed today. While I was in Japan recently, a Japanese pastor told me that he had read the Bible eighty-six times in the past seven years! All too many Christians have scarcely read it through once!

In his letters, Paul did not give the slightest hint that he entertained any doubts of the divine origin and inspiration of Scripture. He had to face, as his Lord had done, all the same textual problems, all the alleged errors and discrepancies in the Old Testament that we have to contend with today. But there is not a scintilla of evidence that these problems ever gave him any concern. We are in good company when we take the same stand.

Paul's confidence in the authority and integrity of Scripture is expressed in these unequivocal terms: "All Scripture is God-breathed and is useful for teaching, rebuking, correcting and training in righteousness, so that the man of God may be thoroughly equipped for every good work" (2 Timothy 3:16). The apostle shared his Lord's conviction that "until heaven and earth disappear, not the smallest letter, not the least stroke of a pen, will by any means disappear from the Law until everything is accomplished" (Matthew 5:18).

> The Scripture is God's Word because it is God-breathed. It originated in His mind, it issued from His mouth, although of course, it was spoken by human authors without destroying either their individuality or its divine authority in the process.
>
> —John Stott

Paul's letters teem with Old Testament references. One diligent Bible student counted a total of 191 Old Testament references in Paul's recorded writings.

Paul was not always careful to quote the exact letter of the original text, but he gave the inner spirit of the message, as guided by the Holy Spirit. Wherever Paul turned in the Scriptures, he discovered principles and truths that precisely fitted his own needs and those of his readers.

Paul's unbounded confidence in the accuracy and reliability of the words of Scripture is apparent. A good example of Paul's careful interpretation of Scripture is his argument on the use of the singular numbers as the object of God's promise. "The promises were spoken to Abraham and to his seed. The Scripture does not say 'and to seeds,' meaning many people, but 'and to your seed,' meaning one person, who is Christ" (Galatians 3:16). In his defense before Felix, Paul declared, "I believe everything that agrees with the Law and that is written in the Prophets" (Acts 24:14).

The apostle believed strongly in the relevance of the Old Testament Scriptures to the life and experience of New Testament Christians. Referring to the experiences of Israel in the wilderness and the judgment that fell on them for their sin, Paul wrote, "These things happened to them as examples and were written down as warnings for us, on whom the fulfillment of the ages has come" (1 Corinthians 10:11). And again Paul applied Scripture to us when he said, "The words 'it was credited to [Abraham]' were written not for him alone, but also for us" (Romans 4:23).

In view of Paul's obvious love and reverence for the Old Testament and the frequent use he made of it, R. E. Speer wrote, "It is pathetic to think that he probably had no copy of his own. The Old Testament Scriptures were in cumbersome rolls, and they were too expensive for individuals to own. On his long journeys Paul could scarcely have carried them with him, if he had been able to purchase them."[3] How greatly we should prize our compact, easily read, and easily carried Bibles!

HANDLING ADVERSE CRITICISM

The higher a man rises in leadership, the more he is open to the criticism and cynicism of rivals or those who oppose his views and actions. The manner in which he reacts will have far-reaching effects on his work. Playing for popularity may mean forfeiting true spiritual leadership.

Paul set a valuable pattern in this regard. Though he wanted to stand well with his fellows, he scorned to do it at the expense of forfeiting the favor of his Lord. He expressed his foremost ambition in 2 Corinthians 5:9: "We make it our goal to please him." In writing to the Galatians, he asked, "Am I now trying to win the approval of men, or of God? Or am I trying to please men? If I were still trying to please men, I would not be a servant of Christ" (Galatians 1:10).

The adverse opinion of his fellows did not disturb Paul unduly, although he did not go out of his way to invite criticism. "I care very little if I am judged by you or by any human court," he wrote to the Corinthians. "Indeed, I do not even judge myself. My conscience is clear, but that does not make me innocent. It is the Lord who judges me. Therefore judge nothing before the appointed time; wait till the Lord comes" (1 Corinthians 4:3-5).

Because Paul knew he was true to the "secret things of God" that had been entrusted to him (1 Corinthians 4:1), he could afford to overlook mere human opinion: "I care very little if I am judged by you." If criticism of the church only thirty years after the Pentecost phenomenon could thus be ignored by the faithful leader, then the censure of the tepid present-day church need hold few terrors for us.

Nor did Paul fear *the world's judgment*—"any human court." Although the world was indeed *not* his judge, he was careful to preserve a balance. He also wrote, "Do not cause anyone to stumble . . . even as I try to please everybody in every way. For I am not seeking my own good but the good of the many, so that they may be saved" (1 Corinthians 10:32-33). Paul did not strain after a wooden consistency, that "hobgoblin of little minds."

"Mendelssohn would as soon have submitted his oratorios to the judgment of a deaf mute, or Raphael his canvas to the judgment of a man born blind," wrote D. M. Panton, "as Paul the mysteries of God to a world that knows not God."

Paul went even further, asserting that the possession of a perfectly clear conscience, invaluable though it is, does not leave one in the clear. Though conscience may flatter us, we must distrust even our own verdict on ourselves because of the subtlety of our hearts. Paul said that he was not the judge. "I do not even judge myself. My conscience is clear, but that does not makes me innocent."

"It is the Lord who judges me," said Paul—and the Lord knows all the information. He can weigh motives as well as assess facts. He is the final court of appeal. His judgment is just and infallible—*therefore we must suspend judgment.* "Judge nothing before the appointed time; wait till the Lord comes." Our powers are too limited, our knowledge so inadequate, our minds too biased to arrive at a correct judgment. We can and must trust all to the Lord's competent hands, and, in the end, "at that time each will receive his praise from God" (1 Corinthians 4:5).

We must keep in mind that indifference to human opinion

can be disastrous if it is not linked with fear of God. And yet some independence of human assessments can be a valuable asset to the disciplined man whose aim is the glory of God. To Paul the voice of man was somewhat faint because his ear was tuned to the more compelling voice of God's appraisal. He did not fear man's judgment because he was conscious that he stood before a higher court.

> Judge not; the workings of his brain
>   And of his heart thou cannot see.
> What looks to thy dim eyes a strain,
>   In God's sight may only be
> A scar brought from some well-won field
>   Where thou wouldst only faint and yield.

An Architect of the Church

The sphere of Paul's leadership was preeminently in the church. Indeed, from the human angle he could be said to be its chief architect. Under the guidance of the Holy Spirit, Paul was largely responsible for fashioning it into the instrument of local fellowship and worldwide evangelism it has subsequently become. He saw clearly that the church was central in God's purposes.

Although in one sense Paul was individualistic, he did not set up some organization of his own in which he was "answerable only to God," as so frequently occurs in our day. He was painfully aware of the weaknesses and failures of the church. Consequently he was resolved to strengthen it from within. His teaching and example give little encouragement to those who try to denigrate the church. "The individualist Christian, therefore, sitting lightly to all Church loyalties, and tempted sometimes to depreciate 'organised Christianity' must expect no sympathy from Paul."[4]

On the Damascus road he began to learn a valuable lesson: Christ places great value on His church. The Lord said, "Saul, Saul, why do you persecute *me?*" (Acts 9:4). He who touched the church touched Christ! Paul came to realize that "Christ loved the church and gave himself up for her" (Ephesians 5:25). In fact, Christ bought the church "with his own blood" (Acts 20:28). It was God's purpose "that now, through the church, the manifold wisdom of God should be made known to the rulers and authorities in the heavenly realms, according to his eternal purpose which he accomplished in Christ Jesus our Lord" (Ephesians 3:10-11).

This high estimate of the church caused Paul to keep it central in thought and planning. It is interesting that many of the figures of speech Paul employs to depict the church are not static, but vital—a living, growing organism rather than a mere organization. Paul saw the church as the mystical body of Christ (Colossians 1:24). In the church he saw unity amid diversity. "Just as each of us has one body with many members, and these members do not all have the same function, so in Christ we who are many form one body, and each member belongs to all the others" (Romans 12:4-5).

Paul's concept of the marital relationship as a picture of the church (Ephesians 5:22-32) is further developed when the church is called *the bride of Christ,* with all the wealth of imagery that figure enshrines (Revelation 19:7; 21:9-10). No more tender and affectionate relationship could be imagined.

Paul did not envision the church as a monolithic institution, but as a warm, caring family—*the family of God,* with all the joyous interrelationships such an ideal family life involves. God who "sets the lonely in families" (Psalm 68:6), sets Christians in churches where, ideally, God's people serve one another and bear one another's burdens. He is "the Father, from whom his whole family in heaven and on earth derives its name" (Ephesians 3:14-15).

The figure of a building, a temple which is in the course of erection, of which Christ is the foundation and chief cornerstone, is also adopted by Paul. It is "a holy temple in the Lord . . . a dwelling in which God lives by his Spirit" (Ephesians 2:21-22). Each new believer is a living stone built into that divine edifice.

The church is also the custodian of the truth of God and the witness to it, for it is "the church of the living God, the pillar and foundation of the truth" (1 Timothy 3:15). Paul nowhere represents the church as faultless or infallible—he knew its weaknesses all too well. When he spoke of Christ presenting His church "as a radiant church, without stain or wrinkle or any other blemish" (Ephesians 5:27), such a day probably seemed far in the future.

While the unity of the church is to be our constant objective and concern, it must not be pursued at the expense of truth. "Unity becomes immoral," wrote R. E. Speer, "when it is purchased at the price of fidelity to Christ or the law of Christ in the life. . . . Only two things were with [Paul] ground for disruption and division. One was disloyalty and unfaithfulness to Christ, and the other, impenitent sin."[5]

The ascended Christ enriched the church with appropriate

spiritual gifts to enable her to fulfill his eternal purpose. But even in her golden days, some of these gifts were being abused. This gave rise to Paul's instructions in 1 Corinthians 12–14 concerning their worthy exercise. He stressed that the purpose of these gifts was for the upbuilding of the possessor. Thus the absence of genuine love would inevitably neutralize their effectiveness.

The apostle Paul had a broad vision for the church. He saw the church as the focal center of worship and witness, of counsel and teaching, of exhortation and encouragement, and of training for service.

THE QUESTION OF CHURCH DISCIPLINE

One of the unwelcome responsibilities of the Christian leader is that of exercising a godly discipline. If scriptural standards and a wholesome moral and spiritual tone are to be maintained in a church or other Christian organization, it is sometimes necessary to exercise a loving and restorative discipline. This is especially the case when doctrinal error or moral failure is involved. Throughout his letters, Paul both encouraged and exemplified the exercise of such discipline.

It is noteworthy, however, that he placed special emphasis on the spirit in which the disciplining is carried out. Harsh and unloving treatment simply alienates the offender, and that is not the purpose in view. "If anyone does not obey our instruction in this letter," Paul wrote, "take special note of him. Do not associate with him, in order that he may feel ashamed. Yet *do not regard him as an enemy, but warn him as a brother*" (2 Thessalonians 3:14-15).

In the case of one who had "caused grief," the Corinthians were exhorted to "forgive and comfort him, so that he will not be overwhelmed by excessive sorrow. I urge you, therefore, *to reaffirm your love for him*" (2 Corinthians 2:5, 7-8).

What should leaders do when someone is overtaken in a sin? "You who are spiritual should *restore him gently*. But watch yourself, or you also may be tempted" (Galatians 6:1). Love is a *sine qua non* in a restoring ministry. It is the person who has faced and honestly dealt with his own sins and failures who is best able to deal sympathetically yet firmly with an offender. A spirit of meekness will achieve far more positive results than a judgmental attitude.

Both Scripture and experience agree that in any disciplinary action the following factors should be given full weight:

(1) Action should be taken only after a very thorough and impartial examination of all the facts has been made. The legal maxim, "Never accept an *ex parte* statement," would apply here.

(2) Genuine love should be the motivation of discipline, and any action should be conducted in the most considerate manner possible.

(3) Discipline should be undertaken only when it is clearly for the overall good of the individual and of the work.

(4) Discipline should be exercised only with much prayer.

(5) The paramount objective of discipline should be the spiritual help and restoration of the person concerned.

Our Civic Responsibility

In the confused and revolutionary world of today, the question of civic responsibility is coming into more and more prominence. Many Christians are being compelled to rethink and redefine their own position in the light of prevailing conditions. Here, too, Paul gives a clear lead.

Living as he did in a totalitarian regime under the jurisdiction of the corrupt Felix and the monstrous Nero, Paul could almost have been excused if he had taken a rather jaundiced view of politics and civil government. Nevertheless he strongly advocated obedience to constituted authority, be it good or bad.

In writing to the Romans, Paul gave strong reasons for his attitude: "Everyone must submit himself to the governing authorities, for there is no authority except that which God has established. The authorities that exist have been established by God. Consequently, he who rebels against the authority is rebelling against what God has instituted, and those who do so will bring judgment on themselves. For rulers hold no terror for those who do right, but for those who do wrong" (Romans 13:1-3). He exhorted Titus likewise to "remind the people to be subject to rulers and authorities, to be obedient, to be ready to do whatever is good" (Titus 3:1-2).

The sound wisdom of this counsel took into account the fact that Paul's fellow countrymen in Rome were a volatile and inflammable group, whose anti-establishment activities, if attributed to Christians, would have had dire results. This was, of course, actually the case when the burning of Rome, of which Christians were entirely innocent, unleashed a fierce wave of persecution against them.

Although unjustly treated by the authorities on several oc-casions, Paul did not encourage either passive resistance or direct action. Christian citizens were to discharge their civil duties, pay taxes, and give respect to authority. "Give every-one what you owe him: If you owe taxes, pay taxes; if revenue, then revenue; if respect, then respect; if honor, then honor" (Romans 13:7).

More than this, Christians had a spiritual responsibility to pray for their rulers. "I urge . . . first of all that requests, prayers, intercession and thanksgiving be made for every-one—*for kings and all those in authority,* that we may live peaceful and quiet lives in all godliness and holiness. This is good, and pleases God our Savior" (1 Timothy 2:1-2). Whether the rulers are worthy of respect or not is irrelevant. Rather, the more unworthy they are, the greater their need for prayer. An appeal to God on behalf of our rulers can make a real differ-ence in the world and in ourselves.

Paul's Roman citizenship was a civil privilege, but he did not always exercise in his own interests the privileges it conferred. But where it was plainly in the best interests of his work Paul did not hesitate to stand upon his rights. His experience in Philippi is a case in point. It took place after a midnight praise session in jail and the subsequent conversion of the jailer.

> When it was daylight, the magistrates sent their officers to the jailer with the order: "Release those men."
>
> The jailer told Paul, "The magistrates have ordered that you and Silas be released. Now you can leave. Go in peace."
>
> But Paul said to the officers: "They beat us publicly without a trial, even though we are Roman citizens, and threw us into

> prison. And now do they want to get rid of us quietly? No! Let
> them come themselves and escort us out."
>
> The officers reported this to the magistrates, and when
> they heard that Paul and Silas were Roman citizens, they were
> alarmed. They came to appease them and escorted them from
> the prison, requesting them to leave the city. (Acts 16:35-39).

In thus asserting his rights, Paul was safeguarding the future interests of the church, which indicates his main concern. His action made it easier for Christians in coming days. The authorities would be much more circumspect after this humiliating experience.

While Paul joyfully submitted to being seized, scourged, and thrown into the inner prison when all might have been avoided by a word, we cannot but admire the moral courage, calm decision, and sound judgment he showed in the calm assertion of his legal rights, precisely when it was most likely to be useful to himself and others. This is enough to show how far he was from putting forth a fanatical or rigorous interpretation on our Savior's principle of non-resistance (Matthew 5:39) which, like many other precepts in the same discourse, teaches us what we should be willing to endure in an extreme case, but without abolishing the right and duty of determine when that case occurs.[6]

This principle is still very applicable in missionary work where the missionary is an expatriate. Paul was no masochist, however, and when nothing significant was at stake, he avoided unnecessary trouble and suffering, "As they stretched him out to flog him, Paul said to the centurion standing there, 'Is it legal for you to flog a Roman citizen who hasn't even been found guilty?'" (Acts 22:25). There were times, however, when he submitted without protest to flogging (2 Corinthians 11:23-24), but in the former case he judged that his suffering would achieve no good purpose.

Later he availed himself of his right to appeal to Caesar, a choice that had far-reaching influence on the future course of the church (Acts 25:8-12). He made his appeal because he saw "that the time had come to determine the status of Christianity before the Roman law."

THE VOICE OF CONSCIENCE

A condemning conscience is no asset to a leader. More than any other New Testament writer, Paul gave clear teaching on the function of conscience—a very important aspect of truth, since it contributes so much to our emotional well-being. Ignorance of its function or persistent disobedience to its dictum can lead to serious spiritual disorders. It is therefore necessary for the leader or counselor to know what the bulk of Scripture has to say on the subject. Paul's frequent references to the state of his conscience indicate the measure of the importance of its proper functioning.

Conscience has been defined as the testimony and judgment of the soul which gives approval or disapproval to the acts of the will. It seems to be a special activity of the intellect and emotions which enables one to distinguish between good and evil—to perceive moral distinctions. Paul said, "I strive always to keep my conscience clear before God and man" (Acts 24:16).

It is this faculty which renders man's sin culpable, and distinguishes him from animals. The word signifies "knowledge held in conjunction with another"—in this instance, with God. It thus carries the idea of man being co-witness with God for or against himself, according to his own estimate of his actions.

Conscience, however, is not an executive faculty. It has no power to make men either do right or cease doing wrong. It delivers its verdict, produces the appropriate emotion, but leaves it to the will of man to act in the light of its judgment. It has no further responsibility. It is like a thermometer, which, though detecting and indicating the temperature, never causes or modifies that temperature. When we obey our conscience, as someone has said, we live in the beatitudes. When we disobey, it cries out like John the Baptist, "It is not lawful!" (Matthew 14:4).

A Condemning Conscience

Paul listed four progressive states of a conscience that condemns:

(1) *A weak conscience is morbid and overscrupulous.* Paul illustrated this from the case of food offered to idols. "Some people are still so accustomed to idols that when they eat such food they think of it as having been sacrificed to an idol, and since their conscience is weak, it is defiled. . . . When you sin against your brothers in this way and wound their weak conscience, you sin against Christ" (1 Corinthians 8:7-12).

This person's conscience seems to react faithfully according to its light, but, like a compass with a weak magnetic current, it tends to vacillate. The result is that its possessor is constantly tormented with doubt concerning the propriety of an action, digging up in unbelief what has been sown in faith. There are perhaps two basic reasons for such weakness: imperfect knowledge of God's Word and will, with a consequently imperfect faith; or an unsurrendered will that causes vacillating actions. The corrective is to face the issues involved clearly in the light of Scripture, to come to a decision according to one's best judgment, and then to resolutely leave it there.

(2) *A weak conscience easily degenerates into a defiled conscience* (1 Corinthians 8:7). If we persist in some action against which conscience has protested, we thereby defile it and prevent its faithful functioning, just as dust clogs the delicate mechanism of a watch, causing it to record the wrong time. This is especially true in the realm of moral purity. "To the pure, all things are pure, but to those who are corrupted and do not believe, nothing is pure. In fact, both their minds and consciences are corrupted" (Titus 1:15).

(3) *A conscience that is disregarded may become habitually evil and guilty,* coming to regard good as evil and evil as good. Paul spoke of "having our hearts sprinkled to cleanse us from a guilty conscience" (Hebrews 10:22). For if the possessor of a guilty conscience is determined to do evil, its protesting voice will grow increasingly faint through the course of time.

(4) *Habitual defiance of conscience reduces it to complete insensitivity,* thus causing it to cease functioning. "Such teachings come through hypocritical liars, whose consciences have been seared as with a hot iron" (1 Timothy 4:2). When conscience becomes cauterized, it no longer protests; consequently no appeal succeeds.

Vice is a monster of such frightful mien
That to be hated, needs but to be seen;
But seen too oft, familiar with her face,
We first endure, then pity, then embrace.
                                    —*Alexander Pope*

Failure to heed the voice of conscience is fraught with serious consequences, Paul warns. We need to hold on "to faith and good conscience. Some have rejected these and so have shipwrecked their faith" (1 Timothy 1:19).

A Commending Conscience

An approving conscience is a prize beyond rubies. Such a conscience is just as faithful in commending the right as in condemning the wrong. "If our [consciences] do not condemn us, we have confidence before God" (1 John 3:21). Paul lists four progressive states of conscience which should be pursued by every believer:

(1) *A clear conscience* is important for spiritual growth. "They must keep hold of the deep truths of the faith with a clear conscience" (1 Timothy 3:9). "I thank God, whom I serve . . . with a clear conscience" (2 Timothy 1:3). A clear or pure conscience is acutely sensitive to the approach of evil. It is kept spiritually clean as we fully obey the light shed on our conduct by the Word of God.

(2) *A good conscience* is the possession of someone who accepts the dictates of righteousness in all things. "The goal of this command is love, which comes from a pure heart and a good

conscience and a sincere faith" (1 Timothy 1:5). We need to hold on "to faith and a good conscience" (1 Timothy 1:19). The reproof of a good conscience is to be welcomed and obeyed.

(3) *A conscience devoid of offense* is vitally important to a Christian. "Herein do I exercise myself, to have always a conscience void of offense toward God, and toward men" (Acts 25:16 KJV). This is the happy state in which no accusing "voice" shatters peace with God, or mars relationships with men. To forfeit this serenity and heart-rest for the sake of some brief gratification is to pay too high a price.

(4) *A perfected conscience*, through the cleansing of the blood of Christ, is a spiritual necessity. "This is a symbol of the present time, during which gifts and sacrifices are offered that cannot perfect the conscience of the worshiper" (Hebrews 9:9 NRSV). "How much more will the blood of Christ . . . purify our conscience" (Hebrews 9:14 NRSV).

Conscience has no cure for its own ills. Thus the provision made in the blood of Christ must be personally appropriated if its owner is to enjoy peace with God.

A conscience is not infallible, but is rather a fluctuating instrument which reacts faithfully to its own accepted standards. The conscience of a Hindu in the past might have protested loudly against the killing of a cow, without at the same time offering any protest at the burning of a widow on a funeral pyre. It is a matter of standard to which conscience bears witness. The consciences of those who conducted the Inquisition inwardly approved their actions, but that did not justify them.

The delicate mechanism of conscience was thrown off balance at the time of mankind's fall. Every conscience now requires adjustment, and will function correctly only when it is adjusted according to the standards of Scripture. Paul asserted that this required strenuous moral effort on his part. "So I strive always to keep my conscience clear before God and man" (Acts 24:16).

Paul himself, blinded earlier in his life by prejudice and bigotry, had reacted to a conscience that was not properly adjusted to Scripture. How bitterly he repented when he opened his eyes to the true nature of the actions which his conscience had approved.

The person who is troubled with a condemning conscience should remember that *with true repentance* the worst sin can be forgiven, passing immediately and completely from the conscience. The Holy Spirit, who delights in applying the cleansing effect of the blood of Christ to the defiled conscience in response to faith, also delights in enabling the believer to walk obediently with a conscience devoid of offense.

THE REALITY OF SPIRITUAL WARFARE

The leader who ignores the activities of our unseen adversary, the devil, has not seriously studied the teachings of Paul on this subject. There is a Chinese proverb that says, "Know your enemy; then in one hundred battles you will be victorious one hundred times." No leader can afford to be illiterate on the subject of the enemy.

The classic passage on the spiritual warfare of the believer with Satan and the powers of darkness—Ephesians

6:10-19—comes from the pen of the apostle. Sagacious leader that he was, he kept alert to the necessity of indoctrinating his followers concerning the foes they would meet. He instructed them in the character and inevitability of spiritual warfare, and in the way to victory. To Paul, the devil was no figment of an overheated imagination, but a wily and experience antagonist. The apostle was too wise to underestimate the caliber of his opponents. He would have approved Victor Hugo's contention that a good general must penetrate the brain of his enemy.

That Paul had done his research on his enemy and was therefore "not unaware of his schemes" (2 Corinthians 2:11), the following verses demonstrate:

Satan himself masquerades as an angel of light. (2 Corinthians 11:14)

You followed the ways of . . . the ruler of the kingdom of the air, the spirit who is now at work in those who are disobedient. (Ephesians 2:2)

The coming of the lawless one will be in accordance with the work of Satan displayed in all kinds of counterfeit miracles, signs and wonders. (2 Thessalonians 2:9)

The god of this age has blinded the minds of unbelievers. (2 Corinthians 4:4)

I am sending you to them to open their eyes and turn them from darkness to light, and from the power of Satan to God. (Acts 26:17-18).

Paul consistently taught that the Christian would inevitably face, in his walk and his witness, the implacable hatred and opposition of both the world and the spiritual forces of darkness. "Our struggle is not against flesh and blood, but against the rulers, against the authorities, against the powers of this dark world and against the spiritual forces of evil in the heavenly realms" (Ephesians 6:12). Paul believed that unseen evil forces rule much of the world, and that these supernatural powers could be vanquished only by the use of supernatural weapons, which he himself employed. He proved a wise and doughty leader in this spiritual warfare.

Satan's power is not inherent, but delegated. Yet although his power is limited, he is more than a match for the strongest Christian. Paul acknowledged that God has granted Satan some measure of control as "the ruler of the kingdom of the air" (Ephesians 2:2). He also indicated that in this warfare there can be no such thing as a pacifist.

True, the warfare is spiritual, but it is desperately real. It is a struggle, a wrestling. Our foes will contest God's eternal purpose at every point, but the Lord is counting on our cooperation. In this late age in world history, we are seeing a fulfillment of Revelation 12:12: "Woe to the earth and the sea, because the devil has gone down to you! He is filled with fury, because he knows that his time is short." He knows that the victory of Christ spells the end of his dominion, and so he is resisting desperately to stave off final defeat.

God's strategy is for all believers to stand fast and hold our ground in the position of privilege and security in which he has placed us. "God raised us up with Christ and seated us with him in the heavenly realms in Christ Jesus" (Ephesians

2:6). Our spiritual responsibility is to "stand . . . stand . . . stand" (Ephesians 6:11, 13-14).

Satan's plan is to dislodge the Christian from this position, driving him to lower levels, forgetful of his privileged position in "the heavenly realms." The deceiver tries to induce the believer to make war with carnal weapons. But Paul warns that spiritual war is not waged the same as other wars. "The weapons we fight with are not the weapons of the world. On the contrary, they have divine power to demolish strongholds" (2 Corinthians 10:4). A bayonet would be a poor weapon against a hydrogen bomb! The fact that it is a spiritual war determines the character of the weapons.

Chained to a soldier as he frequently was, Paul became very conscious of the nature and purpose of armor. He was deeply concerned that his followers should not enter the battle defenseless. So he took up this figure of the armored soldier, thus counseling all Christians to appropriate the divine power and strengthening God has graciously provided. "Be strong in the Lord and in his mighty power" (Ephesians 6:10). It is important for the Christian warrior to don *"the full armor of God."* To omit putting on one piece would leave an Achilles heel exposed.

Because the devil has been a liar from the beginning, the combatant must have *"the belt of truth"* (6:14) buckled around his waist. As the soldier's belt encompassed his waist, holding all the other pieces of armor in place, so the truth of God is to encompass and unify the whole life. This leaves no room for hypocrisy or insincerity.

The function of the breastplate was to protect the vital organs. The Christian soldier must have *"the breastplate of righteousness*" (6:14) in place. Christ provides the righteousness which we must integrate into our own lives. We are to wear integrity as a coat of mail.

In warfare it is important for each soldier to be well shod, or else he will be unable to stand his ground. He is to have "as *shoes for your feet . . .* whatever will make you *ready to proclaim the gospel of peace*" (6:15 NRSV). He must be swift and ready to run with the good news.

The whole length of a soldier's body was protected by a large oblong leather shield, which was saturated with water before battle. The soldier had to hold this shield in place. Paul advised the Christian soldier, "Take up *the shield of faith,* with which you can extinguish all the flaming arrows of the evil one" (6:16). The enemy's arrows, tipped with flaming pitch, would be extinguished when they struck the water-soaked leather.

Satan's arrows can take the form of irrational fears, or sudden and unexpected attacks, especially in the realm of the mind. The exercise of a living, confident faith in our victorious Savior and the intelligent use of the word of God work together to effectually quench the flames of temptation.

"*The helmet of salvation*" (6:17) is the last piece of defensive armor mentioned by Paul, worn to protect the head. An unprotected mind is easy prey to Satan's seductions. If we allow our minds to lie fallow and uncultivated, we are inviting the enemy to sow weeds. It is the mind that Satan seeks to control, because it directs all else. The tragically fallen condition of the world today is mute testimony to the success of his endeavors.

The helmet has to do with our hope. We should be "putting on . . . the hope of salvation as a helmet," the apostle wrote elsewhere (1 Thessalonians 5:8). Christ's salvation brings us hope in a hopeless world. We can be as sure as God is that there is victory for us (1 Corinthians 15:57).

"The sword of the Spirit, which is the word of God" (6:17) is for both defense and offense. It was the major weapon used by our Lord in his epochal conflict with the devil in the wilderness. It proved mightily effective because he knew how to wield it with expertise. It is the spiritual soldier's responsibility to master the word of God so thoroughly, saturating his mind with it, that the Holy Spirit can quickly call to his memory the appropriate truth as a conquering weapon in the moment of need.

There is a self-evident connection between the sword of the Spirit and the communications weaponry of "all prayer" (6:18 KJV). The battle for the minds and souls of men is fought and won primarily in the place of prayer. We are to wage war with *all kinds of prayer,* and each prayer must be *all-out prayer,* for this is total war in which there is no truce.

Thus we see that the purpose of "the full armor of God' is to enable us to stand our ground during times of evil and, after doing all that we should do, to stand victorious over all our foes.

> Soldiers of Christ arise
> And put your armour on,
> Strong in the strength which God supplies
> Through His eternal Son.
>
> Stand then in His great might
> With all His strength endued;
> And take to arm you for the fight
> The panoply of God.

> Leave no unguarded place,
> No weakness of the soul
> Take every virtue, every grace
> And fortify the whole.
>   —*Charles Wesley*

Notes

1. Robertson, A. T., *The Glory of the Ministry* (New York: Revell, 1911), 59.

2. Speer, Robert E., *Master of the Heart* (New York: Revell, 1908), 39.

3. Speer, *Paul, the All-round Man,* 65.

4. White, *Apostle Extraordinary,* 62.

5. Speer, *Paul, the All-round Man,* 65.

6. Speer, *The Man Paul,* 107.

10
DIFFICULT ISSUES

We put up with anything rather than hinder the gospel of Christ.

1 CORINTHIANS 9:12

All of us at times have to decide whether a certain course is right or wrong for us as Christians. Sometimes the problem is not our own, but perhaps we are asked to counsel and guide others in this area. Paul's writings provide us with helpful guidelines in "the gray areas" and in the especially difficult areas of Christian life.

Some interpret Paul's statement, "We are not under law but under grace" (Romans 6:15), as an indication that under the beneficent reign of grace there is no place for the prohibitions and taboos of the Mosaic Law. But this is far from being the case. It is Paul's clear teaching that we are not "under the law" *as a means of our justification,* but that does not mean that we can become lawless for we are under law to Christ, bound by new but no less powerful bonds.

It is a striking fact that every one of the commandments in the Decalogue except, significantly enough, the law concerning the

Sabbath, is repeated in the New Testament. In fact they are repeated with greatly widened scope. For example, our Lord said, "You have heard that it was said, 'Do not commit adultery.' But I tell you that anyone who looks at a woman lustfully has already committed adultery with her in his heart" (Matthew 5:27-28).

We are now under law to Christ, bound by the bonds of love to a new way of life. The genius of the new covenant lies in a unique spiritual fact: Rather than enacting a new set of rules and regulations, it enunciates principles which, when applied correctly, cover every case. The inexorable demands—"Thou shalt . . . thou shalt not"—are replaced by gracious divine undertakings—"I will . . . I will" (Hebrews 8:10-12).

Many vexed anxieties concerning difficult areas of Christian life may be disposed of almost automatically by asking and answering the following questions:

(1) *Is it beneficial and helpful?* "Everything is permissible," Paul writes, "but not everything is beneficial" (1 Corinthians 10:23). Thus, in areas of great concern and uncertainty it is important to consider the following questions: If I take this course, will it tend to make me a better and more mature Christian? Will it make my life more profitable to God and to my fellow man?

(2) *Is it constructive?* Does the pursuit of this particular activity edify and build up the church? "Everything is permissible," Paul tells us, "but not everything is constructive" (1 Corinthians 10:23). Although various pursuits may be legitimate, they are not all of equal value. I should therefore ask myself, Will this course tend to build up my Christian character? Will it equip me for the task of building up the church?

(3) *Will it tend to enslave me?* "Everything is permissible for me," Paul declares, "but I will not be mastered by anything" (1 Corinthians 6:12). Even things quite lawful in themselves can exercise an undue influence, occupying too much of our time, thus holding us back from God's best for us. An undue amount of secular reading or an excessive amount of television viewing, for example, can vitiate our appetite for the Word of God. We have to choose our priorities carefully, even in the area of lawful things.

(4) *Will it strengthen me against temptation?* There is no use praying, "Lead us not into temptation," (Matthew 6:13) if we voluntarily walk right into it. Anything that tends to make sin less culpable or easier to commit must be rejected immediately and resolutely.

This principle does not apply merely to things that are lewd or vulgar. Some things may be intellectual and beautiful, but if our pursuit of them dims our spiritual vision or hinders our running of the race, they are weights which should be laid aside. "Let us throw off everything that hinders" (Hebrews 12:1).

Though different in setting, the problems which confronted the Christians in Rome in Paul's day do not differ essentially from those we face today. Paul's counsel in these areas is strangely contemporary. If we accept and act on the principles he enunciated, we will discover a new and joyous liberty:

(1) *Latitude of judgment in the gray areas*—"One man's faith allows him to eat everything, but another man, whose faith is weak, eats only vegetables. The man who eats everything must

not look down on him who does not, and the man who does not eat everything must not condemn the man who does, for God has accepted him" (Romans 14:2-3). The problem under discussion in this passage is food offered to idols. Paul pointed out that a well-taught Christian does not consider an idol to have any spiritual reality in itself; thus this mature believer feels free to eat food that has been offered to the idol. But to someone who is weak in faith, it is a stumbling block.

Since no vital doctrine was at stake, Paul urged tolerance in these kinds of situations with significant potential for friction. Within the church, in matters which are not clearly erroneous or those which are merely cultural, there is room for genuine differences of opinion, and we should uphold the right of our brother to entertain opinions contrary to our own.

(2) *The right of personal conviction*—"One man considers one day more sacred than another; another man considers every day alike. Each one should be fully convinced in his own mind" (Romans 14:5).

It is easy to be like the chameleon, changing our theological color to suit our company. It is easy to be swayed by doctrinal preference or prejudice rather than influenced by the clear teaching of Scripture. Paul instructs us to come to clear convictions of our own that are squarely based on Scripture, not allowing our decisions or conduct to be dictated by someone else. We have to live with the outcome of our decisions, so we should make sure they are based on solid, biblically informed convictions.

(3) *Accountability to God alone*—Paul asks, "Who are you to judge someone else's servant? To his own master he stands or

falls." And a little later the apostle continues, "So then, each of us will give an account of himself to God" (Romans 14:4, 12). Because we are all members of society, we have certain social responsibilities. But we are ultimately answerable to God alone.

One alone is our Master; no one else can claim for himself God's sovereign rights over us. The certainty that the judgment seat lies ahead for all believers should deeply influence our conduct. "You, then, why do you judge your brother?" Paul asks. "Or why do you look down on your brother? For we will all stand before God's judgment seat" (Romans 14:10).

(4) *Absence of a critical spirit*—It is not our prerogative to criticize or judge our brother's actions; that right belongs to God alone. "Therefore let us stop passing judgment on one another. Instead, make up your mind not to put any stumbling block or obstacle in your brother's way" (Romans 14:13). In the last day we will be judged by God, not by one another. Thus, we should always credit others with the same degree of equity and sincerity as we would expect them to accord to us.

(5) *Abstinence in the interests of others*—We should not live for our own pleasure alone, absorbed solely in our own interests. We must take into account the possible effects of our lives on others. Accordingly, "It is better not to eat meat or drink wine or to do anything else that will cause your brother to fall" (Romans 14:21).

The freedom some Christians claim for social or moderate drinking has often proved to be the downfall of the weaker brother who does not have the same strength of will. It is our responsibility to voluntarily limit our own legitimate enjoyment in the interests of weaker brothers and sisters. "We who are strong ought to bear with the failings of the weak and not to please ourselves" (Romans 15:1).

(6) *Abstinence from things of doubtful legitimacy*—The very fact that we have doubts raises the presumption that the practice under review is questionable. All our actions should carry the positive assurance of faith.

"Blessed is the man who does not condemn himself by what he approves. But the man who has doubts is condemned if he eats, because his eating is not from faith; and everything that does not come from faith is sin" (Romans 14:22-23). The presence of continuing doubt should be regarded as a call to delay action until clearer light emerges. Through prayer and study of relevant Scriptures, the Holy Spirit will either remove the doubt or give the conviction that this action is not the will of God.

On the other hand, our problem might be that we have a weak or uninstructed conscience that needs education by the Word of God. It is very possible that, as a result of our background and past associations or because of tradition or prejudice, we may have doubts about things the Bible does not condemn. In such matters we should depend on the gracious ministry of the Holy Spirit to guide us into all truth (John 16:13).

How to Handle Money

Paul preserved for us a powerfully relevant saying of our Lord: "The Lord Jesus himself said, 'It is more blessed to give than to receive'" (Acts 20:35). It can be said with certainty that Paul himself qualified for the beatitude he commended.

In no area did the apostle exercise more meticulous care than in the sensitive area of finances. In this area he set an important example for the Christian leader. Probably more leaders have lost spiritual power due to wrong attitudes and actions when dealing with money than through any other single cause.

Our Lord accorded an astonishing prominence to money in his teaching. In one way or another, it entered into one verse out of six in the Synoptic Gospels and into sixteen of his thirty-eight parables. Jesus Christ thus recognized that money is one of the central realities of life from the cradle to the grave. It is one of the dominating topics of conversation and one of the most absorbing objects of pursuit. Money is a subject on which one cannot be neutral.

Paul was very conscious of this ubiquitous problem, and was therefore scrupulous in his financial dealings and his stewardship. In order to remove from the young churches the burden of his support he earned his own living, and at times he supported his colleagues as well. He was "financially clean," setting a noble example of generosity.

Paul stated his financial philosophy in 1 Timothy 6:5-10, referring to "men of corrupt mind, who have been robbed of the truth and who think that godliness is a means to financial gain. But godliness with contentment is great gain. For we brought nothing into the world, and we can take nothing out of it. But if we have food and clothing, we will be content with that. People who want to get rich fall into temptation and a trap and into many foolish and harmful desires that plunge men into ruin and destruction. For the love of money is a root of all kinds of evil. Some people, eager for money, have wandered from the faith and pierced themselves with many griefs."

This is, alas, a sad biographical description of too many Christians, leaders included. For this reason Paul warned the young pastor Timothy, who was about to undertake his new assignment, to beware of potential monetary problems.

Paul was careful not to assume too much personal responsibility in the financial matters of the early churches. When the Corinthian Christians collected money for their needy friends in Jerusalem, he would not assume the responsibility of taking the gift. He felt that the donors should be the ones to take it to the recipients and thus he would be clear of any suspicion of financial dishonesty.

Systematic and proportionate giving was encouraged by the apostle. "On the first day of every week," Paul counseled the Corinthians, "each one of you should set aside a sum of money in keeping with his income, saving it up, so that when I come no collections will have to be made. Then, when I arrive, I will give letters of introduction to the men you approve and send them with your gift to Jerusalem. If it seems advisable for me to go also, they will accompany me" (1 Corinthians 16:2-4).

This procedure shows true sagacity, for in new and developing churches in areas of a low standard of living the stewardship of money collected often proves a real temptation to the one with the financial responsibility. For this reason, it is always wise for more than one person to be involved in the counting and stewardship of money.

As he was stimulating the Corinthian church to greater generosity, Paul cited the infinite generosity of the One who for our sakes became poor (2 Corinthians 8:9), and also the lavish liberality of the poor Macedonian church: "Out of the most severe trial, their overflowing joy and their extreme poverty welled up in rich generosity. For I testified that they gave as much as they were able, and even beyond their ability. Entirely on their own, they urgently pleaded with us for the privilege of sharing in this service to the saints" (2 Corinthians 8:2-5).

Here is a unique type of fund raising, in which the donor begs for the opportunity to give to the cause! (compare Exodus 35). The Macedonians demonstrated very clearly that it is more blessed to give than to receive.

KNOWING THE WILL OF GOD

There is no area in which a leader requires greater spiritual wisdom than in that of spiritual guidance—discerning the will and leading of God in any situation. Those who are not leaders may think that a broader experience and a longer walk with God inevitably results in much greater ease in discerning the will of God in perplexing situations. This is by no means always the case.

It seems that God's method is usually, to the contrary, to leave more and more to the leader's spiritual judgment and to give even fewer sensory and tangible evidences of His guidance than in earlier years. Perplexity in gaining clear direction can add to the many pressures incidental to any responsible office. Paul's experience provides us some extremely valuable lessons in guidance.

Though he had responded immediately to the call of God

on the Damascus road, Paul's career as a missionary did not commence until he had been working for a while with the church at Antioch some ten or eleven years later.

While the multiracial leaders of the church were "worshiping the Lord and fasting, the Holy Spirit said, 'Set apart for me Barnabas and Saul for the work to which I have called them'" (Acts 13:2). This divine summons marked the real beginning of Paul's missionary career. To his ardent spirit, those previous years of preparation must have dragged on like a glacier of time. At last he was to be set free, sent forth on his world mission.

Paul did not embark on his missionary career until his personal call—"I *have called* them," were the words of the Spirit—was confirmed to the local church with which he was associated (at Antioch), and then confirmed *by* them. "So after they had fasted and prayed, they placed their hands on them and sent them off" (Acts 13:3). Thus the *corporate* guidance of the church leaders confirmed Paul's *personal* guidance.

The Antioch church thus established a precedent that could well serve as a model for churches today. It means a great deal to both the church and the missionary if the individual's call is ratified by the leaders of his home church.

It is of significant interest that Paul, although he was already superbly trained, served for a period with a more experienced worker from the church which sent him out, not only during his first term of missionary service but also through part of the second. But what a senior missionary he was privileged to serve under! Barnabas, "the Son of Encouragement"! (Acts 4:36). Without doubt this godly, large-hearted man exercised a great influence on Paul during those training days.

And it says a great deal for Barnabas that he showed no apparent trace of resentment or jealousy when his junior partner streaked way ahead of him, assuming leadership of team, as was inevitable sooner or later.

A Scripture passage which illustrates God's method of guidance in a very helpful way is Acts 16:6-10. In order to interpret this passage, we have to bear in mind that the call from Macedonia is not to be regarded as an *initial missionary call,* but rather as a divine method of redirecting certain people, who had already responded to the initial call, into a specific sphere of worship. It was the Holy Spirit who chose the time and place of service for Paul and his colleagues.

From this passage we learn that God guides at times by inward warnings or prohibitions. "Paul and his companions traveled throughout the region of Phrygia and Galatia, having been kept by the Holy Spirit from preaching the Word in the province of Asia. When they came to the border of Mysia, they tried to enter Bithynia, but the Spirit of Jesus would not allow them to. So they passed by Mysia and went down to Troas."

Asia and Bithynia were to hear the Word later, but at this time the divine strategy was that the good news should travel westward. The winds of the Spirit were blowing in Europe, which had recently become ripe for harvest. Paul and his band were to be privileged to put in the sickle.

Being spiritually sensitive, Paul responded to the restraint of the Spirit, and did not press forward in self-will. Instead he drew aside to Troas to discover in prayer and consultation with his companions the geographical will of God for them. The tiny band scarcely realized the world-shaking consequences that hung on their decision!

The issue before them was clear: either go back home or push forward and cross the sea. How could they know which was God's will? God did not leave them long in doubt. The negative guidance of closed doors was followed by positive direction.

"During the night Paul had vision of a man of Macedonia standing and begging him, 'Come over to Macedonia and help us'" (16:9). Note that the vision came to Paul *after* he had gone forward in obedience to the Great Commission, and that it formed only one element in his guidance. He had already completed his first assignment, and was now reaching out to "the great unreached."

Even after the vision, Paul as the leader was careful to check his guidance with his colleagues, including them in any decisions that needed to be made. After Paul had taken all these steps, they were brought to a Spirit-wrought unity of mind. "After Paul had seen the vision, we got ready at once to leave for Macedonia, concluding that God had called us to preach the gospel to them" (16:10). A. T. Robertson sees in this mutual consultation "a good illustration of the proper use of reason in connection with revelation, to decide whether it is a revelation of God, to find out what it means for us and see that we obey the revelation."[1]

Thus, before taking a further step, he assured himself that his vision was in line with the Word of God, was witnessed to by the Holy Spirit, was agreeable to his companions, and was approved by his own judgment. This system of checks and balances saved him from regret and dismay when he later met a hostile reception and they found themselves with bleeding backs in the jail at Philippi. Instead of doubting the validity of their guidance when things seemed to go wrong, they turned to prayer and praise. How could the devil defeat such men?

DETERMINING OUR RIGHTS

One factor that contributed greatly to Paul's spiritual stature and colored his leadership skill was his attitude toward his rights. In a day when far greater emphasis is laid on claiming one's obligations, Paul's attitude administers a wholesome contemporary corrective. The leader must be very sensitive in this area if he is to exercise a growing influence.

In 1 Corinthians 9, a chapter which gives in part the secret of Paul's soul-winning ministry, he referred seven times to his rights *in the context of the gospel.* This piece of autobiography carries a powerful message for the person who wants to become an effective soul-winner and leader.

If someone is to reach these goals, it is obvious that he must achieve victory over the *wrong* things in his life. But not every Christian worker recognizes that this process may entail the renunciation of things that in themselves are *right.* In this enterprise, Paul set a shining example. Referring to his right to church support, he claimed, "We put up with anything rather than hinder the gospel of Christ" (9:12). It is the small man who is *always* asserting his rights.

Paul recognized that, although certain things may be legitimate in themselves, they may well limit his ministry. As we have seen, he had just previously written, "'Everything is permissible for me'—but not everything is beneficial. 'Everything is permissible for me'—but I will not be mastered by anything" (6:12). Later in the letter he wrote, "'Everything is permissible'—but not everything is constructive" (10:23). Paul knew it was very possible to indulge in legitimate tastes and appetites to an inordinate degree, thus becoming enslaved. There must be victory in the realm of legitimate desire, as well as in that of illegitimate indulgence.

Oswald Chambers maintained in his trenchant style, "If we are willing to give up only *wrong* things for Jesus, let us never talk about being in love with Him. Anyone will give up wrong things if he knows how. But are we prepared to give up the best we have for Jesus Christ? The only right a Christian has is the right to give up his rights." In order to be the best we can be for God, we need to make some voluntary renunciations (Luke 14:33). If we wish to scale the heights for God, we must face up to this challenge of voluntary renunciation.

Our Exemplar in this area of sacrifice, as in everything else, is our Lord himself. As "heir of all things" (Hebrews 1:2), he had enjoyed and exercised rights beyond our wildest imaginations. And yet for our sakes he renounced them one by one. The renunciation of rights began when he arose from his eternal throne and "forsook the courts of everlasting day, and chose with us a darksome house of mortal clay" (Milton).

The greatest sacrifice can be rendered by those who have the most to surrender. Christ forsook the congenial company of angels for the hostility of men, the comforts of home for the life of an itinerant, the riches of heaven for the poverty of earth. And, finally, in love he renounced what could have been a somewhat comfortable place among the tribe of humanity by suffering the pangs of death as a criminal.

If sacrifice is indeed the ecstasy of giving the best we have to the one we love the most, it inevitably follows that there will often be simple, mundane rights as well that must be renounced for love of our Lord.

If I pay my fare on a bus, I have an inalienable right to a seat if there is one available. But when a tired mother with a baby in one arm and parcels in the other enters a crowded bus, although no one can challenge my right to a seat, I have the higher right and responsibility to waive that right and offer my seat to the lady. And shall we do less for our Lord?

In 1 Corinthians 9, Paul asserts his right to three realms: the right to gratify hunger for food and drink (9:4); the right to a normal marital life (9:5); the right to financial support from the church (9:6-12).

To Paul the joy and obligation of sharing the gospel was vastly more important than gratifying his appetite or indulging in some desire for outside financial support. Although he was no ascetic, he was truly determined that he would not be dominated by his body.

"I will not be bossed by appetite," said John Wesley. So for two years he lived on a diet of potatoes! It was this inflexible purpose to be the best for God that gave Wesley such a tremendous influence on his own generation. "We did not use this right," Paul claimed (9:12).

For love of Christ and in the interests of soul-winning effectiveness, Paul sacrificed his rights to be accompanied by a wife. "Not to make full use of my rights in the gospel" (9:18 NRSV), was his characteristic attitude. He did not squeeze the last drop out of his rights.

Paul strongly asserted his right to be supported by those to whom he ministered. "The Lord has commanded that those who preach the gospel should receive their living from the gospel. But I have not used any of these rights" (9:14-15). Paul did not want to be lumped with the greedy priesthood; furthermore he desired to maintain financial independence in the exercise of his apostolic authority. So he elected to support himself by his trade of tentmaking. However, on some rare occasions he accepted gifts from churches.

It takes uncommonly strong motivation to induce a leader or anyone else to adopt this attitude to his rights. "Though I am free and belong to no man," wrote Paul, "I make myself a slave to everyone, to win as many as possible" (9:19). And a slave has *no* rights!

A missionary in China said of his experiences, "When I came to China I was all ready to *eat bitterness* [Chinese idiom for 'suffering hardship'] and like it. That hasn't troubled me particularly. It takes a little time to get your palate and your digestion used to Chinese food, of course, but that was no harder than I expected. Another thing, however"—and he paused significantly—"*another thing* that I had never thought about came up to make trouble. I had to *eat loss!* [Chinese idiom for 'suffering the infringement of one's rights']. I found that I couldn't stand up for my rights—that I couldn't even *have* any rights. I found that I had to give them up, every one, and that was the hardest thing of all." In the words of Jesus, he had to "deny himself" (Luke 9:23) and that is never easy. But, "This is the way the Master went, should not the servant tread it still?"

THE ISSUE OF SLAVERY

The charge has been leveled against Paul that he should have waged a stronger protest against the ghastly slave traffic of his day. But the charge will not stick. He is blamed for appearing to accept the slavery of Onesimus without protest, rather than telling Philemon, the slave owner, that slavery is inconsistent with Christian principles. But if we sincerely endeavor to put ourselves in Paul's situation, we will more readily understand the reason why he did not assume the role of a revolutionary crusader.

When Paul said to Philemon that he should regard Onesimus "no longer as a slave, but better than a slave, as a dear brother" (Philemon 16), "He laid a foundation for a new order that was bound to come."[2]

Gibbon, the noted historian, estimated that in A.D. 57 one half of the population of the Roman Empire were slaves. Thus the question of the status of slaves was an extremely important social issue in the church of that day. Moreover, the manner in which Paul handled this issue has significant lessons for the leaders of today.

In the culture of those days, slaves were not considered to be persons, but merely possessions. Their status was no higher than that of animals. The literature of that period portrays the inhuman cruelty with which many slaves were treated. There were many, on the other hand, who received very humane treatment.

One could well imagine a firebrand like Paul springing into the arena, setting up a strong anti-slavery movement, and inflaming the slaves against their masters. But the manner in which he handled this hot issue has caused some to conclude that he approved of slavery and was rather insensitive to social injustice. This was far from being the case. Guided by the Holy Spirit, Paul adopted a method which, amid the prevailing conditions of that day, was superbly calculated to achieve the amelioration of the lot of the slave.

The apostle's counsel to Timothy was eminently wise for the circumstances he faced. A successful social revolution would have required such a vast network of organization that it could never have been achieved overnight. Any attempt to do so would have brought untold disrepute and persecution to the young Christian movement. So Paul advised Timothy, "All who are under the yoke of slavery should consider their masters worthy of full respect, so that God's name and our teaching may not be slandered" (1 Timothy 6:1).

Insubordination was out of the question for the Christian slave. Instead, he was to be content with his lot. "Were you a slave when you were called? Don't let it trouble you—although if you can gain your freedom, do so. For he who was a slave when he was called by the Lord is the Lord's freedman; similarly, he who was a free man when he was called is Christ's slave" (1 Corinthians 7:21-22). Paul thus called on the Christian slave to rejoice in the spiritual blessing and freedom which faith in Christ had brought to him.

It is interesting to observe that Paul uttered a note of warning against the impertinent or undue familiarity of slaves toward their Christian masters—something that could have easily taken place. "Those who have believing masters are not to show less respect for them because they are brothers. Instead, they are to serve them even better, because those who benefit from their service are believers, and dear to them" (1 Timothy 6:2).

Paul told Titus, "Teach slaves to be subject to their masters in everything, to try to please them, not to talk back to them, and not to steal from them, but to show that they can be fully trusted, so that in every way they will make the teaching about God our Savior attractive" (Titus 2:9-10).

And what about the duty of the master to the slaves? It was not left unaddressed by Paul. "Masters, treat your slaves in the same way. Do not threaten them, since you know that he who is both their Master and yours is in heaven, and there is no favoritism with him" (Ephesians 6:9).

Those who question Paul's concern for slaves should remember that it was in the church that the liberation of the slaves began. For within the church Paul enunciated and enforced principles that if acted upon would strike off their shackles. He taught the emancipating message of equality in Christ. "There is neither Jew nor Greek, slave nor free, male nor female, for you are all one in Christ Jesus" (Galatians 3:28). Brotherly love must characterize all Christian relationships. "Be devoted to one another in brotherly love. Honor one another above yourselves" (Romans 12:10). Both masters and slaves must respect their mutual rights and perform their mutual duties (Ephesians 6:5-9).

As the church grew in numbers and these principles were increasingly practiced, the seeds of social reform began to germinate, and gradually enlightenment came. Under Christian emperors, slavery began to dwindle. The reform process was slow, but wherever Christianity has entered, slavery has exited. Christianity and slavery can never live together in peaceful coexistence.

A Unique View on Suffering

The leader must have his own well-developed philosophy on the problem of suffering, for he will frequently be called upon to counsel those who find themselves in the crucible. Paul could urge his young colleague, "Take your share of suffering" (2 Timothy 1:8 NEB) because he himself was prepared to do the same, setting the example.

Alexander the Great's veterans threatened mutiny on the grounds that he was indifferent to their hardships and their wounds. But he sprang up on the dais and said to the disgruntled men, "Come, now, who of you have wounds, let him bare himself and I will show mine. No member of my body is without its wounds. I have been wounded by the sword, by the arrow from the bow, by the missile from the catapult. I have been pelted with stones and pounded with clubs while leading you to victory and glory."[3]

Paul, a greater conqueror than Alexander the Great, could make this same statement. "Let no one cause me trouble," he challenged his opponents, "for I bear on my body the marks of Jesus" (Galatians 6:17).

More than any other apostle, Paul was exposed to suffering, hardship, and distress. The catalogue of his trials, which he reluctantly cataloged in 2 Corinthians 11:23-28, seems more than any human being could survive. And yet he emerged triumphant, more than a conqueror (Romans 8:37).

We can discover Paul's philosophy of suffering from one incident in his own experience. Perhaps more than any other apostle, Paul had been granted special revelations by the Lord. Referring to one such incident he wrote, "Although there is nothing to be gained, I will go on to visions and revelations from the Lord. I know a man in Christ who fourteen years ago was caught up to the third heaven . . . . And I know that this man . . . was caught up to paradise. He heard inexpressible things, things that man is not permitted to tell" (2 Corinthians 12:1-4).

These were no ordinary experiences. Indeed, they were so unique that they presented Paul with a great temptation to feel pride. God was deeply concerned that Paul might succumb to this temptation, thus limiting his ministry. So the Lord introduced an equalizing factor: "'To keep me from becoming conceited because of these surpassingly great revelations, there was given me a thorn in my flesh, a messenger of Satan, to torment me'" (12:7).

Paul was strangely reticent about the exact nature of the thorn. Concerning its nature, opinion is sharply divided. Some think it was *mental or spiritual*—sensual desires, depression, or doubt. Others think that it was *physical*—epilepsy, malaria, or ophthalmia (inflammation of the eye). The fact that it was a thorn or stake "in the flesh" would weight the scales in favor of the latter. Whatever it was, we should be grateful for the apostle's studied reticence, for we can now confidently apply the divine remedy to our own particular thorns.

We should be grateful, too, that this experience provided the occasion for the enunciation by the Lord of a classic spiritual principle: "My grace is sufficient for you, for my power is made perfect in weakness" (12:9). Here is a divine assurance that, even if the painful situation—the thorn, whatever it may be—is not removed, there is always enough compensating grace available.

This painful and humiliating experience was part of the price of Paul's service to God, part of his equipment for his office. In spite of his brilliant gifts, had it not been for the presence of this infirmity in Paul's life, in all probability he would never have achieved his dynamic ministry for the Lord.

While we do not know the nature of the thorn, there are certain facts we do know, which can be of great value in meeting suffering, whether our own or that of others:

(1) Paul's thorn was something that continued over a significant period of time.

(2) It was the subject of repeated but unanswered prayer. "Three times I pleaded with the Lord to take it away from me," he stated (12:8).

(3) It was an instrument of humility—"to keep me from becoming conceited" (12:7). It deflated Paul's ego and sapped him of self-reliance.

(4) Paul's thorn afforded Satan the perfect opportunity for tormenting him (12:7). Peter was not the only apostle whom the Lord permitted Satan to sift (Luke 22:31). The devil meant it for evil but our God "turned the curse into a blessing" (Deuteronomy 23:5).

(5) It became a channel of grace. "My grace is sufficient for you" (2 Corinthians 12:9). Rather than remedying the thorn by removal, God gave his compensating grace. The answer came not by subtraction, but by addition; not in God granting a more congenial task or a changed location, but in Paul's

appropriation of God's more than sufficient grace where and as he was. "To multiplied trials, He addeth more grace."

(6) The thorn provided an opportunity for rejoicing in weakness. "Therefore I will boast all the more gladly about my weaknesses. . . . For Christ's sake, I delight in weaknesses. . . . For when I am weak, then I am strong" (12:9-10).

(7) It provided a backdrop for displaying Christ's power—"so that Christ's power may rest on me" (12:9). In this verse, the word *my* should be omitted, so that Paul's statement is simply, "Power is made perfect in weakness."

Paul thus mastered the art of turning a debilitating weakness into a glorious triumph. He learned that what he had at first regarded as a restricting handicap was in reality a heavenly asset—the road to an enlarged ministry centered in the Lord. Thus his weakness became a potent weapon.

> I asked the Lord that He should give success
> To the high task I sought for Him to do;
> I asked that every hindrance might grow less
> And that my hours of weakness might be few;
> I asked that far and lofty heights be scaled—
> And now I humbly thank Him that I failed.
> For with the pain and sorrow came to me
> A dower of tenderness in act and thought,
> And with the failure came a sympathy,
> An insight which success had never brought.

Father, I had been foolish and unblest
If Thou hadst granted me my blind request.

Paul's attitude to this disciplinary experience was exemplary. Note that he did not say, "A thorn was *imposed* on me," but, "There was *given* me"—as a gift of grace. The thorn did not remain a messenger of Satan to torment him, but became a gift of God's grace to prepare the way for a wider ministry.

THE PRECIOUS COMMODITY OF TIME

Time is one of the leader's most valuable raw materials. For one's use of time determines not only the amount of work one achieves but also its quality.

Time is not given, but purchased. Some such thought lies behind Paul's cryptic words in Ephesians 5:16—"Redeeming the time" (KJV), or "Buy up your opportunities" (Weymouth). Time is opportunity, and it becomes ours only by purchase. There is a price to be paid for its most strategic employment. We exchange our time in the marketplace of life for certain occupations or activities. J. B. Phillips adds another angle: "Make the best use of your time," exchanging it only for the things of greatest value.

Time is a stewardship of which we must render account. The value of our contribution to our generation will depend on how we strategically use it. Each moment is a gift of God, thus it should not be wasted. Because it is our most valuable possession, we should develop a critical conscience in this area.

Time can be *lost* as well as redeemed. And it is solemnizing to remember that lost time can never be recalled. Time cannot be *hoarded;* it must be fully spent each day. It cannot be *postponed,* it is now or never. If not used productively, time is irretrievably lost.

Paul's mastery of time can be measured by the amount of ministry he achieved in his lifetime. Following his extensive journeys on a map and hearing of his hard work and adventures leaves us almost breathless. If we, too, are to experience successful leadership, the mastery of *our* time will be a matter of prime importance.

Like his Master, Paul selected his priorities with great care, allowing no time for endeavors that were not vital. His life demonstrated that strength of moral character develops through *rejection of the unimportant.*

In this age of high technology and high pressure, it is instructive for us to note that the apostle seemed to accept pressures and interruptions as normal routine. And few things generate more pressures than those caused by insufficient time.

"We do not want you to be uninformed, brothers," he wrote, "about the hardships we suffered in the providence of Asia. *We were under great pressure,* far beyond our ability to endure, so that we despaired even of life. Indeed, in our hearts we felt the sentence of death" (2 Corinthians 1:8-9). He realized that, according to God's plan for his life, these things had been foreseen; thus there was no reason for them to disillusion him.

To the alert Christian, interruptions are divinely interjected opportunities. And Paul was convinced that his life had been divinely planned: "We are God's workmanship, created in Christ Jesus to do good works, which God prepared in advance for us to do" (Ephesians 2:10). It is possible for us, through prayer and communion, to discover the unfolding pattern for each day.

In seeking to plan our time to the best advantage, it may be helpful to bear the following suggestions in mind:

(1) Everyone has been entrusted with the same amount of time.

(2) God's plan leaves sufficient time for the fulfillment of all His will for each day.

(3) He expects of us daily only what is reasonable and achievable.

(4) When we select our priorities carefully, they should not conflict with our obvious duties.

(5) The conflicts and pressures we experience usually arise as we confuse human desires or pressures—either our own or those of someone else—with the duties God expects us to fulfill.

(6) Time is too valuable to be spent on secondary matters when primary matters are screaming for attention.

(7) "I didn't have time," is usually the unconscious confession of someone who is making a wrong choice of priorities.

Few things bring the conscientious Christian worker into bondage more thoroughly than this matter of the strategic employment of his time. For many people, time seems to be perennially in short supply. It is necessary, therefore, either to come to terms with it or to work under perpetual tension and strain. After all, there will always be great areas of unmet needs, even after we have conscientiously done all in our power to meet our obligations.

By careful and prayerful selection of priorities, *we should make each half-hour carry its own quota of usefulness,* and then commit the rest to God. Our real problem is not in the *amount* of time available, but in its strategic employment, for which we are indisputably responsible. A wise use of time involves firm purpose and strict self-discipline, but it can be done if we *will* to do it.

Our responsibility extends only to those things which lie within our own control. Not every call for help is a call from God. It is manifestly impossible to respond to every appeal for aid. We must remember that circumstances beyond our control are no cause for self-accusation.

Every leader should, however, honestly face the question: Am I using my time for what matters most, or am I dissipating some of it on matters of secondary importance? The best way to answer the question is to conduct a strict analysis of the way we fill our time in any one week. This exercise might bring some surprises.

Paul challenged the Corinthians, "Follow my example, as I follow the example of Christ" (1 Corinthians 11:1), a challenge few of us would care to put forth. In his use of time, Paul modeled his own life on the life of his Lord. How very much both of them managed to crowd into their days!

Taking time for disciplined recreation and relaxation

should not be regarded a matter of secondary importance. The leader who makes provision for the renewal of physical and nervous resources is not merely engaged in trifles. Jesus took His disciples aside for rest and relaxation. He himself sat down and rested on the well when He was weary after a busy day of ministry.

Our Lord did not drive His tired body relentlessly onward. Had He done so, He would have missed the prepared heart of the needy woman by the well. Jesus was not an ascetic who refused to enter into the normal social life of the people. He did not consider it time wasted when He attended the wedding feast.

Failure to take adequate time for relaxation may prove counter-productive. Of course we must always be ready to have our recreation time interrupted if the interests of the kingdom so demand. It must always be, "Kingdom first, self second."

When the saintly young revivalist Robert Murray Mc-Cheyne lay on his deathbed at the age of twenty-nine, he said to the friend by his side, "God gave me a horse to ride and a message to deliver. Alas, I have killed the horse, and now I cannot deliver the message!" There is no virtue in flogging the horse unmercifully. But perhaps that is not our trouble. Maybe our horse needs the spurs!

A perusal of the Gospels leaves one with the impression that the Master walked through life with a measured and un-hurried tread. He never seemed harassed, though He was perpetually thronged. He managed to make people feel that He had time for everyone.

Wherein lay the secret of Jesus' serenity? I believe it lay in

His assurance that He was walking in step with His Father's time-plan—a plan drawn so accurately that every hour was accounted for. He allowed no one to advance or retard His time-schedule. He arranged His calendar each day in communion with His Father. Each day He received the words to say and the works to do, and this made Him serene in the midst of crowding duties. "The words I say to you are not just my own. Rather, it is the Father, living in me, who is doing his work" (John 14:10).

Jesus moved about with consciousness that there was a divine timing for the events of His life, and His concern was to complete the task committed to Him in the allotted time. When His brothers were pressing Him to publicize himself, He made a revealing statement: "The right time for me has not yet come; for you any time is right" (John 7:6). He refused to live a haphazard life, for that would mar His Father's plan. Paul modeled his life on that of his Master; we, too, are called to that same commitment.

But to effect a radical change in our time habits will require dependence on the Lord's enabling. Not all of us have inflexible wills, as Paul appeared to have; but we can all be "strengthened in [our] inner being with power through his Spirit" for this purpose (Ephesians 3:16 NRSV). Paul gave Timothy the helpful assurance that "God did not give us a spirit of cowardice, but a spirit of power and of love and of *self-discipline*" (2 Timothy 1:7). A. T. Robertson says that this refers to the human spirit as endowed by the Holy Spirit, on whose cooperation we can indeed count.

The use of our time depends on the pressure of motive. Is our motivation sufficiently compelling to counter our erroneous and long-indulged time habits? Only true dedication to the Lord, as well as time itself, will tell.

Notes

1. Robertson, A. T., *Word Pictures of the New Testament* (New York: Harpers, 1930), 248.

2. Rall, Henry F., *According to Paul* (New York: Scribners, 1944), 215.

3. Macartney, *The Greatest Men of the Bible,* 18.

11

THE ROLE OF WOMEN

There is neither . . . male nor female . . . in Christ Jesus.

GALATIANS 3:28

Since women constitute probably more than one-half of the membership of the universal church, an understanding of Paul's view on the role of women in the church is of vital importance. With the rise of the women's liberation movement, the basis of which is cultural rather than biblical, attitudes have become more strongly polarized than ever before.

In our increasingly egalitarian society, it is not easy to view all that the Scriptures have to say on the subject of women in an objective and unprejudiced manner, for our views have been shaped by long-term tradition. No doubt only in eternity will there be a true consensus.

The problem is all the more sensitive because godly and scholarly teachers fervently espouse opposing views. For this reason, undue dogmatism would be out of place. And so I present my view with due humility and respect for the many sincerely held views within the church.

I do not take an extreme position, nor do I contend for a dominant position for women, either in the realm of leadership or in that of theology. Although "there is neither . . . male nor female" (Galatians 3:28) in Christ, Scripture does recognize certain differences in the roles of men and women in the church. Certainly Paul would not advocate the unisex ideas of our age. And yet he did consider there to be valid scriptural grounds for according women a much wider and more influential place in the life and ministry of the church than had traditionally been the case. This subject is, of course, too wide for full treatment in small compass, but it is my objective to support this view from Scripture.

A Misunderstood Apostle

In this day of strident contention for women's rights, Paul is often in the firing line, receiving much flak because of his alleged denigration of the role and status of women. "Maligned on the one hand, exonerated on the other, Paul himself is lost behind a barrage of claim and counterclaim."[1]

Frequently the apostle is dismissed as a frustrated male chauvinist, venting his spleen on women in general. But those who level these charges against him have either never read the relevant Scripture passages carefully and objectively, or have read them with jaundiced eyes, for they will not carry any such interpretation.

It would be difficult to fault Paul in his general attitude toward women, marriage, and the family. In his contacts with his hostesses, audiences, and female members of his teams, he was uniformly chivalrous and brotherly. He never hinted at or asserted any superiority of men over women. In his letters he expressed the highest regard and esteem for his female colleagues, commending them as his fellow workers in the gospel without any discrimination between them and the male members of the team.

Paul went far beyond the traditional position accorded to Jewish women, who in the synagogue worship were segregated and silent. For he upheld their right to pray and prophesy in the church, provided their heads were covered. "Every woman who prays or prophesies with her head uncovered dishonors her head—it is just as though her head were shaved" (1 Corinthians 11:5). If the relevant texts are read in the context of the times in which they were written, it will be discovered that in his day, far from being a male chauvinist, Paul was a foremost champion of women's rights. He would have been regarded by his contemporaries as distinctly *avant garde*.

As we appraise his attitude and teaching, we must keep the cultural climate of his times in view. We need only compare his outlook and practice with those of the leaders and founders of the other religions to see the great superiority of his conception of the status of women, as compared with that of Buddhism, Hinduism, and Islam. Instead of excoriating Paul, Christian women should be lauding his championship, for it has paved the way for so many blessings and privileges they now enjoy.

The case has been well stated by George Matheson: "One of the most distinctive elements in Paul's Christian experience was the recognition of the claims of women; in nothing is he more sharply distinguished from his Jewish countrymen. Even those passages in which he seems to depreciate, are dictated by a precisely opposite motive—the desire to conserve for women that distinctive and peculiar sphere of which Jewish politics deprived her."[2]

In interpreting Paul's teaching on this subject, the following facts should be borne in mind. First, he was answering specific questions addressed to him by the local church at Corinth, relating to particular problems that were troubling them. Second, he wrote at a time when prevailing conditions were both perilous and precarious. This fact emerges from his answer in 1 Corinthians 7:25-27 (NRSV): "Now concerning virgins, I have no command of the Lord, but I give my opinion as one who by the Lord's mercy is trustworthy. I think that *in view of the impending crisis,* it is well for you to remain as you are. Are you bound to a wife? Do not seek to be free." Third in the Gentile cities where the Christians lived, immorality was rife. Thus it was especially important for Christian women to comport themselves in church in such a manner that was above criticism.

It would seem that, in this specific statement, Paul was not legislating for all times and circumstances, but giving specific advice for the difficult days immediately ahead. The apostle was simply saying that people would be wise not to change their present status, in view of existing conditions. If this interpretation is correct, and I believe it is, then improved conditions would allow for elasticity in the implementation of his advice.

A LOOK AT THE SCRIPTURES

Where there are clear, unambiguous scriptural statements they are to be obeyed without reservation. But on this subject of the role of women in the church, the wide divergence of views held by equally sincere persons indicates that many of these Scriptures are by no means clear and unambiguous. On this point J. I. Packer, an evangelical scholar of repute, wrote:

> Though all Paul's commands being apostolic carried the authority of the Lord whose ambassador Paul was, that does not rule out the possibility that some of them were *ad hoc* enactments, responses to particular situations which would become dead letters if the situation changed. It is arguable that the command that women should not teach but keep silent is a case in point: a prudential rule of thumb applying the creation pattern to a situation where converted pagan ladies, uneducated and brought up to think of themselves as inferior beings, had now discovered their dignity under God in Christ and it was now going to their heads.
>
> In that case it is the principle and not the rule of thumb that has abiding authority, and it is conceivable that under a difficult cultural background where Christian women were not under the same temptations to wildness, a relaxed rule could serve the principle equally well.[3]

This principle of interpretation throws light on three important passages concerning which there is a strong polarization of views:

> Now I want you to realize that the head of every man is Christ, and the head of the woman is man, and the head of Christ is God. Every man who prays or prophesies with his head covered dishonors his head. And every woman who prays or

prophesies with her head uncovered dishonors her head—it is just as though her head were shaved. If a woman does not cover her head, she should have her hair cut off; and if it is a disgrace for a woman to have her hair cut or shaved off, she should cover her head. (1 Corinthians 11:3-6)

God is not a God of disorder but of peace.

As in all the congregations of the saints, women should remain silent in the churches. They are not allowed to speak, but must be in submission, as the Law says. If they want to inquire about something, they should ask their own husbands at home; for it is disgraceful for a woman to speak in the church. (1 Corinthians 14:33-35)

I want men everywhere to lift up holy hands in prayer, without anger or disputing.

I also want women to dress modestly, with decency and propriety, not with braided hair or gold or pearls or expensive clothes, but with good deeds, appropriate for women who profess to worship God.

A woman should learn in quietness and full submission. I do not permit a woman to teach or to have authority over a man; she must be silent. For Adam was formed first, then Eve. And Adam was not the one deceived; it was the woman who was deceived and became a sinner. (1 Timothy 2:8-14)

Interpreters on the extreme right maintain that these passages impose an absolute prohibition on any teaching or leadership role for women in the church. Some even go so far as to prohibit them from praying at gatherings where men are present. The spiritual barrenness and frustration that often results from such an extreme position is a plain matter of fact throughout church history.

Those on the extreme left interpret these passages as solely reflecting the contemporary cultural situations of that age, having no parallel today and only marginal relevance. They therefore accord to women a rather unlimited teaching and leadership role in the church.

But are these two extremes the only possible interpretations? May there not be a reasonable alternative position, an acceptable *via media*? Since both Scripture and Paul have so much to say about women, the family, and marriage, isn't it rather unlikely that the problem can be resolved by quoting two or three passages, while largely ignoring a much greater body of Scripture? For there has indeed been a rather ill-balanced emphasis on the negative in the passages quoted above, and inadequate attention paid to many other passages that make a somewhat more liberal interpretation possible.

Paul's lofty conception of the sanctity of the marriage bond is reflected in the parallel he draws between the relation of man and wife and the relation of Christ and the church. "Husbands, love your wives, just as Christ loved the church and gave himself up for her . . ." (Ephesians 5:25). This is in striking contrast to the teaching of the Koran or the Confucian classics, in which the emphasis is invariably on the duty of the wife to the husband.

Such subjugation was not so with Paul. "Husbands ought to love their wives as their own bodies. He who loves his wife loves himself" (Ephesians 5:28). It should be noted, too, that the subjection of the woman to the man is to her own husband, not to all men.

THE CULTURAL FACTOR

The question inevitably arises: How much should the existing cultural situation in Paul's day be taken into account as we try to determine a contemporary application? In this connection, F. F. Bruce makes a pertinent comment: "Cultural relativity is certainly to be reckoned with when the permanent message of the New Testament receives our practical attention today. The locale and temporary situation in which that message was first delivered must be appreciated if we are to discern what its permanent essence really is, and learn to apply it in the local and temporary circumstances of our own culture."

In 1 Corinthians 11:1-15, Paul is concerned with a question of church order: the advisability of women veiling their heads in public worship services at Corinth. In this passage he is not making a proclamation about teaching for all time.

It has been pointed out that the sentence, "I do not permit a woman to teach or to have authority over a man," appears timeless in English, as if he were saying, "I would *never* allow a woman to teach . . ." (1 Timothy 2:12). However, in the Greek there is a present active verb here which can be translated, "I am not presently permitting a woman to teach or to have authority over a man." Paul was apparently prohibiting those who were not properly instructed from teaching. The teacher must first be taught. But the verb tense cannot necessarily be made into a general principle for all time.[4]

What cultural conditions prevailed at that time which should be taken into account in our interpretation?

- Almost half the people in the Roman Empire were slaves.
- The status of women was very low. They were mostly uneducated and were regarded as chattels.
- In their prayers, Jewish men thanked God that they were not women.
- Men were not supposed to speak to women in public places.
- Eastern women did not go out with their heads uncovered. To do so, or to have their heads shaved marked them as immoral.
- In worship in the synagogues, women were segregated from the men, and they often interrupted their husbands by asking them questions better answered at home.

Practically none of these cultural conditions find a parallel in the culture of our day. The cross of Christ has brought about a vast change in the status of women.

When existing conditions are taken into consideration, we see that the restrictions Paul made were reasonable and necessary. But are they equally applicable in the cultural milieu of our own times? What were guiding lines for worshipers in one church and cultural situations should not be turned into binding laws for all times and all situations.

Paul's restrictions were aimed at correcting improprieties and bringing order in very disturbed church gatherings

(1 Corinthians 14:33), not at placing a blanket ban on women praying, prophesying, evangelizing, or teaching. His emphasis is on women conducting themselves so blamelessly that their behavior neither disrupts the worship service nor shames their husbands. Paul was discouraging public questioning or arguing in cases where wives were usurping authority over their husbands, thus disgracing them.

Although I admit the undoubtedly difficult problems of interpretation of these passages, there are other considerations that lead me to doubt that the traditionally restrictive attitude is the true and only possible explanation.

The Holy Spirit sovereignly bestows spiritual gifts on each believer without reference to gender (1 Corinthians 12:11). These gifts are clearly to be used for the upbuilding of the church. Had the Spirit withheld these gifts of teaching or leadership from women, we would accept that as a clear indication of His will. But He had not done so.

If men alone are appointed to positions where these gifts may be exercised, is not the purpose of the Spirit's gifts being frustrated and the church being impoverished? "The Spirit of God has expressly endowed some women in both the Old and New Testaments with powers of leadership, as though to show that He reserves this right, even though the vast majority of leaders have been men."[5]

Both the Bible (Old and New Testaments) and various accounts of church history (past and present) provide examples of godly women exercising a fruitful ministry in prophecy, administration, evangelism, and teaching. Where there is a wooden adherence to Pauline prohibitions in today's changed situations, sterility and frustration very often result. On the other hand, the undoubted spiritual release and fruitfulness that has followed the ministry of such women as Catherine Booth, Ruth Paxson, Henrietta Meares, Geraldine Howard Taylor, Isabel Kuhn, and many others has to be accounted for if the restrictive interpretation is the correct one.

It is true that the New Testament does not depict women in a dominant role in either theology or leadership. But there is a great deal apart from those roles that women did in the early church, and may still do—often better than men.

Hudson Taylor was a pioneer not only in the use of lay people in missionary work but also in the use of single women in pioneer work in China. In 1885, the China Inland Mission opened centers on the populous Kwang Sin River that were conducted by single women. Thirty years later there was a complete chain of ten central stations, sixty outstations, over 2,200 communicants, and large numbers of enquirers, pupils in schools, etc. Those ladies were still the only foreign missionaries alongside the native pastors whom they had trained.

In view of this remarkable achievement from Christian women, one cannot but ask, Does the Holy Spirit speak with two voices—bidding women not to teach or lead, and then richly blessing them when they disobey?

If it is objected, "But we must go by Scripture and not by experience," the objection is valid. *But* we must make sure that we have *rightly interpreted Scripture.* In this case, the presumption surely is that this is not the correct interpretation. More than sixty percent of the missionaries today are women, most of whom exercise the functions which the extremely conservative position would deny them. Without their contribution in teaching and often in leadership, the missionary cause would be immeasurably impoverished.

NAMING SOME OF THE WOMEN OF GOD

Paul apparently saw no discrepancy between the instructions he gave and the fact that in his time women did pray, prophesy, teach, and evangelize. He numbered many women among his friends and fellow workers, and was warm in his praise and appreciation of their sacrificial service.

In Romans 16, Paul gave special mention to almost as many women as to men friends, and the expressions he used throw some light on the role and ministry of women in those early days of the church.

Phoebe (16:1-2) is described as a "deacon." In the Greek language, the word *deacon* is the same whether in the masculine or feminine gender. It is the same word Paul used of himself and Apollos (1 Corinthians 3:5), and there are no linguistic or theological grounds for differentiating between their function and that of other male deacons. The word is used as often with women as with men. As A. G. Stewart commented, it seems that women were doing as much of the work required of deacons as were the men, whether they were given the title or not.

In verse 2, the word translated "help" further elucidates her function. Cognate terms from the same root are applied to those who exercised leadership in the churches, for example, "those . . . who are over you in the Lord" (1 Thessalonians 5:12). In Romans 12:8 the same word is rendered "leader," and in 1 Timothy 5:17 it is applied to "the elders who direct the affairs of the church." Thus the term used by Paul could indicate that Phoebe not only fulfilled the function of deacon but also had some administrative role.

Priscilla (16:3) appears to have been more dynamic than her husband Aquila, but together they functioned as a husband-wife pastoral team, conducting a church in their homes at Corinth and Rome. That she exercised a teaching ministry is explicitly cited in Scripture (Acts 18:26), for she and her husband took the eloquent Apollos to their home and thoroughly explained the way of God. There is no suggestion that in doing so Priscilla was acting contrary to Paul's teaching. She shared with Aquila the title and task of "fellow worker." Paul described the indebtedness of "all the churches of the Gentiles" to their joint ministry. (16:4).

Junias (16:7) was stated to be a woman by both Chrysostom and Theophylact. Ancient commentators concluded that Andronicus and Junias were a married couple. Junias is not found elsewhere as a man's name. Of Junias, Chrysostom wrote, "Indeed to be apostles at all is a great thing. But to be even among these of note just consider what a great encomium this is. But they were of note owing to their works, to their achievements. Oh! How great is the devotion of this woman that she should be even counted worthy of the appellation of apostle."[6]

In verse 7, we are told that Andronicus and Junias were "outstanding among the *apostles*," using that word, of course, in its secondary sense, as of Barnabas (Acts 14:14). Although there is no absolute certainty, there are reasonable grounds for regarding Junias as an apostle in the limited sense.

Philip's daughters (Acts 21:9) were referred to by Eusebius as "mighty luminaries." They clearly exercised the prophetic gift.

In 1 Corinthians 11:5, Paul gave instructions on how

women should be attired while praying or prophesying. In that context there is no distinction made between the praying and prophesying of the men (11:4) and that of the women (11:5). In each Scripture passage where Paul listed spiritual gifts, prophecy is given the prime position as the most important gift, and in 1 Corinthians 14:3, he specifies its nature and function: "Everyone who prophesies speaks to men for their strengthening, encouragement and comfort." Would it not be strange for Paul to permit women to exercise the higher gift of prophecy, yet forbid them the less important gift of teaching?

Euodia and Syntyche (Philippians 4:2-3) apparently held positions of leadership so influential in the church that their disagreement endangered its unity. Although not condoning their estrangement, Paul commended them most warmly. They "contended at [Paul's] side in the cause of the gospel" (4:3), sharing the common task and ministry. He identified them with Clement and the other fellow workers in the proclamation of the gospel.

All these scriptural passages, when taken together, comprise a good case for maintaining that the command to keep silence in the early church was not absolute. The Bible makes it clear that women were not precluded from exercising a fruitful and fulfilling ministry.

In 2 Timothy 2:2, Paul wrote, "The things you have heard me say in the presence of many witnesses entrust to reliable men who will also be qualified to teach others." In point of fact, *men* here is a generic term that could be equally rendered "faithful persons," a term that could include women.

That some women today have a gift for teaching and applying the Bible can hardly be denied. This would seem to be one measure of the difference between our situation and Paul's when there was no New Testament to teach! But the giving of the gift is itself an indication that God meant the gift to be used in the Church for edification. *Prima facie,* then, God intends some women to teach and preach.[7]

In the light of what has been written, Paul appears to accord to women a satisfying, if not dominant role in the realms of prayer, teaching, evangelizing, and administration. As stated earlier, there is no scriptural precedent for women holding a dominant role in leadership or in theology. But in his administration of the universal church and the execution of the Great Commission, the Holy Spirit has given a much wider scope of ministry to women than is usually accorded to them in our churches. Do we have a valid reason for being more selective than the Holy Spirit?

Notes

1. Williams, Don, *Paul and Women in the Church* (Glendale: Gospel Light, 1977), 11.

2. Speer, *The Man Paul,* 104.

3. *Evangelicals and the Ordination of Women* (Kent: Grove Books, 1973), 24.

4. Williams, *Paul and Women in the Church ,* 112.

5. *Evangelicals and the Ordination of Women,* 21.

6. Sanday, William, and Arthur Headlam, *The Epistle to the Romans* (Edinburg: T. & T. Clark, 1902), 423.

7. *Evangelicals and the Ordination of Women,* 25.

12

A PHILOSOPHY OF WEAKNESS

He said to me, "My grace is sufficient for you, for my power is made perfect in weakness." Therefore I will boast all the more gladly about my weaknesses, so that Christ's power may rest on me.

2 CORINTHIANS 12:9

We form part of a generation that worships power—military, intellectual, economic, scientific. The concept of power is worked into the warp and woof of our daily living. Our entire world is divided into power blocs. Men everywhere are striving for power in various realms, often with questionable motivation.

On the subject of power there is a stark and startling contrast between God's outlook and our own. His words through Isaiah in his day are no less appropriate in our own: "My thoughts are not your thoughts, neither are your ways my ways" (Isaiah 55:8). Unlike every worldly philosophy, the gospel seeks out the weak and the poor.

The celebrated Scottish preacher James S. Stewart made a statement that is both revolutionary and challenging, because it strikes such a shrewd blow at our human pride and self-sufficiency: "It is always upon human weakness and humiliation, not human strength and confidence, that God chooses to build His Kingdom; and that he can use us not merely in spite of our ordinariness and helplessness and disqualifying infirmities, but precisely because of them. It is a thrilling discovery to make, and it can revolutionise our missionary outlook."[1]

These words are indeed revolutionary, but no more so than Paul's own philosophy of weakness. Note some of the apostle's paradoxical statements:

"God chose the weak things of the world to shame the strong. . . . I came to you in weakness and fear, and with much trembling. . . . I delight in weakness . . . . For when I am weak then I am strong. . . . 'My power is made perfect in weakness.' . . . I will not boast about myself, except about my weaknesses" (1 Corinthians 1:27; 2:3; 2 Corinthians 12:10, 9, 5).

Just as these surprising passages enshrine one of the master principles of Paul's leadership, they should be a major part of ours. The appreciation of weakness is a complete reversal of the thinking of the worldly mind, challenging its accepted standards. Who in the world would consider weakness a leadership quality? But Paul had learned that "the foolishness of God" (activities that seem foolish to unregenerate people) "is wiser than man's wisdom, and the weakness of God" (operations of God that to men seem weak and futile) "is stronger than man's strength" (1 Corinthians 1:25).

God is a God who hides himself; His power is usually hidden power. He often conceals His omnipotence under a mantle of silence. Who notices the tons of sap being forced through the wood of the great tree trunk? How silently and unnoticeably water becomes ice! Surely His weakness is greater than our power.

The hidden wisdom and power of God is seen, Paul says, in the kind of people He chooses to establish His kingdom. "Not many of you were wise by human standards; not many were influential; not many were of noble birth. But God chose the foolish things of the world to shame the wise; God chose the weak things of the world to shame the strong . . . so that no one may boast before him" (1 Corinthians 1:26-29).

"It must not be forgotten," wrote A. T. Robertson, "that Jesus chose His disciples from the unschooled artisans and fishermen of Galilee, save Judas the Judean. He passed by the rabbinical theological seminaries where religious impulse had died and thought had crystallised. He will pass by the schools of today if the teachers and students close their minds to Him."[2]

Although Paul himself was an intellectual he gloried in the fact that God had purposefully not chosen the intellectual, highborn, powerful, and influential. Instead He chose people who were weak in ability, influence, or even in body—those discarded and disregarded by the world—to achieve his purposes of blessing. And the reason for his choice? "So that no one may boast before him" (1:29).

Dr. Stewart sees in our very human weaknesses a potentially powerful divine weapon. "Nothing can defeat a church or soul that takes not its strength but its weakness, and offers that to be God's weapon. It was the way of William Carey and Francis Xavier and Paul the apostle. 'Lord, here is my human weakness: I dedicate it to Thee for Thy glory!' This is the strategy to which there is no retort. This is the victory that overcomes the world."[3]

We must remember that God does not confine himself to weak and despised nonentities! The Countess of Huntingdon, referring to 1 Corinthians 1:26, used to say, "I am so thankful for one letter in the Bible; it does not say 'not *any* noble,' but 'not *many* noble.'" God desires to bless and use *all* His children irrespective of accidents of birth, native talent, or charm of disposition. But He can do so only when they are willing to renounce total dependence on their own natural gifts and qualifications.

It is Paul's contention that God can achieve His purposes most effectively either in the absence of human wisdom, power, and resources, or in the abandonment of reliance on them. Human weakness provides the best background for the display of God's great power, and so it is a valuable asset.

Paul himself was one of the wise, noble, and influential men of his day. He possessed intellectual power, emotional ardor, fiery zeal, and irresistible logic; and yet he renounced dependence on these qualities and on all the artifices at his command. Note the spirit in which he approached his ministry to the Corinthian church: "I came to you in weakness and fear, and with much trembling. My message and my preaching were not with wise and persuasive words, but with a demonstration of the Spirit's power." (1 Corinthians 2:3-4).

Even while Paul was making use of his gifts and qualifications, he was inwardly renouncing dependence on them to achieve spiritual results, relying instead on the ungrieved Holy Spirit to supply the power. He welcomed the weakness that made his dependence on God more complete.

Dwight L. Moody, the Billy Graham of his day, learned to exploit the power of weakness as Paul did. He was innocent of education, his physical appearance was unattractive, and his voice was high-pitched and nasal. But his conscious weakness did not prevent God from shaking the world through him.

On one occasion, a press reporter was assigned to cover his campaigns in order to discover the secret of his extraordinary power and influence over people of all social strata. After he returned from his assignment, he wrote, "I can see nothing whatever in Moody to account for his marvelous work."

When Moody was told this, he chuckled, "Of course not, because the work was God's, not mine." Moody's weakness was God's weapon.

Paul's "thorn in the flesh" was a perpetual reminder of his human weakness, but he realized that it was by no means purposeless: it was "so that Christ's power may rest on me" (2 Corinthians 12:9). James Denney wrote in this connection, "No one who saw this [power] and looked at a preacher like Paul could dream the explanation lay in him. Not in an ugly little Jew, without presence, without eloquence, without the means to bribe or to compel, could the source of such courage, the source of such transformations, be found; it must be sought, not in him but in God."[4]

It is unlikely that Paul relished his weakness from the very beginning of his ministry. Like us, he was disposed to protest, and so it was a gradual learning process. He said, "*I have learned* to be content whatever the circumstances" (Philippians 4:11). But as he mastered the divine law of compensation, he ultimately reached the high ground of being able to say in sincerity, "I *delight* in weaknesses, in insults, in hardships, in persecutions, in difficulties. For when I am weak, then I am strong" (2 Corinthians 12:10).

One great secret of Paul's success as a leader was that he set a glowing example for his followers, for he extracted power from his weaknesses. He wrested their secrets from them, and through the Spirit's ministry discovered that they could become an asset, rather than a liability.

Are we not inclined to regard our weakness and inadequacy as justifiable excuse for shrinking from a difficult assignment? God advances these very qualities as the impetus for tackling it. If we maintain that we are too weak, he asserts that very weakness as the reason he chose us, so that his strength can be perfected in our weakness. It was said of the heroes of faith of Hebrews 11 that "their weakness was turned to strength" (11:34 NEB).

At the very beginning of the China Inland Mission, in January 1866, Hudson Taylor expressed his philosophy of weakness: "We may adopt the language of the Apostle Paul and say, 'Who is sufficient for these things?' Utter weakness in ourselves, we should be overwhelmed with the immensity of the work before us, and the weight of responsibility laying upon us, were it not that our very weakness and insufficiency gives us special claim to the fulfillment of HIS promise who has said, 'My grace is sufficient for thee; my strength is made perfect in weakness.'" Over a hundred years later, the mission founded by Hudson Taylor is still proving the validity and power of this philosophy.

Notes

1. Stewart, James S., *Thine Is the Kingdom* (Edinburgh: St. Andrews Press), 23.

2. Robertson, A. T., *The Glory of the Ministry* (New York: Revell, 1911), 253.

3. Stewart, *Thine Is the Kingdom*, 24.

4. Denney, James, *Expositor's Bible—Corinthians* (London: Hodders), 160.

13

THE TRAINING OF
OTHER LEADERS

*Set an example for the believers in speech, in life,
in love, in faith, and in purity.*

1 TIMOTHY 4:12

I t was John R. Mott's contention that leaders must seek to
multiply their own lives by developing younger men, by
giving them full play and adequate outlet for their powers. In order to achieve that, heavy burdens of responsibility
should be laid on them, including increasing opportunities of
initiative and power of final decision. Moreover, they should be
given recognition and generous credit for their achievements.

Paul's method of preparing Timothy for his lifework was
deeply instructive. Paul trod in the steps of his Master, and his
teaching techniques were fully in harmony with Mott's pre-
scription. He poured his own personality and convictions into
Timothy, and was prepared to spend much time with him.

Timothy was probably about twenty years of age when his

tutelage began. The young man of God apparently lacked the assertiveness of his teacher, a weakness which was probably accentuated by his poor health. "He was more prone to lean than to lead." His innate timidity and tendency to self-pity also needed correction. The young fellow needed more iron built into his character. From incidental references it could be inferred that Timothy tended to be overly tolerant and partial with important people, and quite desultory in his work.

From Paul's exhortation to "stir into flame the gift of God" (2 Timothy 1:6 NEB), it appears that, like many others, Timothy was apt to rely on old spiritual experiences, instead of rekindling their dying embers.

In spite of these minuses in Timothy's makeup, Paul cherished a high opinion of his potential, with very lofty and exacting aspirations for him. He held him to the highest standard, not sparing him difficult experiences. Nor did he shelter him from hardships that would toughen his fiber and impart virility.

Paul assigned Timothy tasks far above his conscious ability, but encouraged and fortified him in their execution. How else could a young man develop his powers and capacities than by tackling situations that extend him to the limit?

A great deal of Timothy's training was received on the job as he traveled with Paul—a unique privilege for so young a man. Such travels brought him into contact with all kinds of people—men of stature whose personalities and achievements would kindle in him a wholesome ambition. From his tutor he no doubt learned how to meet triumphantly the reverses and crises that seemed routine in Paul's life and ministry.

Paul was quick to share his ministry with his colleagues.

He entrusted Timothy with responsibility for establishing the Christian nucleus at Thessalonica and confirming them in the faith, a task for which he earned Paul's approval. He was also sent as troubleshooter to Corinth, a hot spot where Paul's apostolic authority was under fire. There Timothy learned invaluable lessons in the process. As usual, Paul's exacting standards, high expectations, and heavy demands served to bring out the best in the young man, saving him from the peril of mediocrity.

Great men are made more by their families than by their successes. Abraham Lincoln, it has been said, "is perhaps the best-known example. He was a failure in business; he was a failure as a lawyer; he failed to become a candidate for the State legislature. He was thwarted in his attempt to be a Commissioner of the General Land Office. He was defeated in his bids for vice-presidency and Senate. But he didn't let failure ruin his life. Nor did he allow failure to embitter him toward people."

In an era when a man of under thirty years of age was not normally considered worthy of much recognition, Timothy's youthfulness was a distinct handicap. But that did not prevent Paul from giving him responsibility and encouraging him not to be dismayed because of his age.

"Don't let anyone look down on you because you are young," he counseled, "but set an example for the believers in speech, in life, in love, in faith and in purity" (1 Timothy 4:12). These are qualities in which a young person is apt to be deficient.

But exemplary living can largely offset any disadvantage of youthfulness. A young man said to me at a center for Christian work, "You have to have gray hair to give out a hymn book in here!" The secretary of the movement was over eighty! Paul teaches us the important lesson that is wise to entrust promising and stable young people with reasonable responsibility earlier, rather than later.

THE CHARGE OF PAUL

Paul concentrated his counsel to Timothy in a fourfold charge, and buttressed it with five "trustworthy sayings." In order to encourage and fortify the young pastor for his daunting task at Ephesus—a church that had enjoyed a galaxy of talent, and for which Timothy would have felt utterly inadequate—Paul addressed four solemn charges to him from which we can learn what things he deemed vitally important in pastoral work.

Guard the Deposit

"Timothy, guard what has been entrusted to your care. Turn away from godless chatter and the opposing ideas of what is falsely called knowledge, which some have professed and in so doing have wandered from the faith" (1 Timothy 6:20-21).

Moffatt translates the first part of this passage, "Keep the securities of the faith intact." This is an illustration from banking, and the word sometimes translated as "deposit" had much the same significance then as it does today—money entrusted to a banker for safekeeping. It is the duty of the banker to hand it back intact. Thus Paul was saying to Timothy, "God has made a deposit in your spiritual bank; stand guard over it."

Timothy had been entrusted with God's salvation truths,

and he would have to give an account of his stewardship. He needed to use his spiritual gifts to the best possible advantage in advancing the kingdom. He had been chosen to be a herald to sound out the Word. "Of this gospel I was appointed as herald," Paul himself claimed (2 Timothy 1:11). One who proclaims the Word must be sure to keep the deposit intact. He must not only defend the faith against the attacks of false teachers, but also preach it positively with conviction.

In our justifiable reaction to an unloving judgmentalism in the church, we must not become so tolerant that we fail to guard the deposit. But we do need to contend for the faith without being contentious in spirit.

Act without Favoritism

"I charge you, in the sight of God and Christ Jesus and the elect angels, to keep these instructions without partiality, and to do nothing out of favoritism" (1 Timothy 5:21). Did this charge spring from Paul's fear that young Timothy might be too easily influenced by pressure groups—a situation which is not unknown in Christian work in our own day?

We are all at times liable to be moved by subjective considerations, and so we need the stiffening influence of this grave charge. In Christian work absolute impartiality and unimpeachable honesty and integrity are essential. Our own personal aversions or affinities must be laid aside. The words *partiality* and *favoritism* both imply prejudice—a prejudging of the case. Even worldly men expect fairness and impartiality. But certainly the church should set the standard, since its well-being is dependent on an impartial discipline.

Keep the Principles Stainless

"I charge you to keep this commandment without spot or blame until the appearing of our Lord Jesus Christ, which God will bring about in his own time" (1 Timothy 6:13-15). The word *keep* means "to preserve, to stand guard over." It would seem that Paul was urging Timothy to keep the commission entrusted to him, the principles enshrined in the word of God, unsullied and flawless until the appearing of Christ.

A leader is the guardian of the principles of the church, mission, or organization in which he carries responsibility. It is for him to practice, teach, and cherish these principles, seeing to it that they are conscientiously observed by those under his care.

Keep Your Sense of Urgency

"In the presence of God and of Christ Jesus, who will judge the living and the dead, and in view of his appearing and his kingdom, I give you this charge: Preach the Word; be prepared in season and out of season; correct, rebuke and encourage" (2 Timothy 4:1-2). It should be borne in mind that Paul was anticipating an early demise, and was therefore often under the influence of the world to come. His charge concerning the coming judgment must have seemed especially solemn to his young colleague.

"Herald the Word. Proclaim it in all its glory and completeness," he urged. "Be ready whether the opportunity seems favorable or unfavorable, convenient or inconvenient. Buy up every opportunity. Never lose your sense of urgency. Take the initiative and press forward with unflagging zeal." The old warrior had earned the right to pass on these charges to the younger man, for he had demonstrated them as a seasoned spiritual veteran to a unique degree in his own life and ministry.

Some Trustworthy Sayings

In his pastoral letters, Paul wrote to encourage and brace his young colleagues. He recounted five "trustworthy sayings" in these letters, each of which deals with important aspects of Christian life and service. By using the formula, "Here is a trustworthy saying" which deserves full acceptance, he was drawing attention to the messages which were apparently current in the churches of that day. But these sayings still have relevance today to the church.

Salvation

"Here is a trustworthy saying that deserves full acceptance: Christ Jesus came into the world to save sinners—of whom I am the worst" (1 Timothy 1:15). This saying epitomizes the gospel. It is a startling but simple epigram that has stood the fiery test of challenge and experience. It has emerged from the crucible of ridicule and persecution with luster undimmed, and should therefore command spontaneous and enthusiastic assent.

Paul used the words *came into the world* not merely to express change of location but also to emphasize change of state and environment. The supreme sacrifice is implied: *to save sinners.* The more Paul grasped the magnitude of the sacrifice of Christ and the grace of God, the deeper was his consciousness of his own unworthiness—"of whom I am the worst."

Leadership

"Here is a trustworthy saying: If anyone sets his heart on being an overseer, he desires a noble task" (1 Timothy 3:1). The *New English Bible* renders it, "To aspire to leadership is an honourable ambition." It should be noted that the honor or nobility is in the task itself, not in the prestige it may confer.

It may well be asked, "Doesn't this saying tend to encourage unworthy or sinful ambition—"the last infirmity of noble minds"? Shouldn't the office seek the man, rather than the man the office?

Yes and no! Today the office of bishop or overseer is prestigious, but when Paul wrote these words, it involved a great degree of sacrifice and danger and very little prestige. To assume this office in the church was to invite persecution, hardship, and even death—even as it does in many lands today. This would surely tend to prevent applications by insincere candidates. Under the circumstances of those days, strong incentive was needed to encourage the right type of person to take office, and Paul was seeking to provide this incentive.

Sanctification

"God . . . saved us through the washing of rebirth and renewal by the Holy Spirit, whom he poured out on us generously through Jesus Christ our Savior, so that, having been justified by his grace, we might become heirs having the hope of eternal life. This is a trustworthy saying. And I want you to stress these things" (Titus 3:4-8).

What things was the young leader Titus to stress? First, he was to emphasize the philanthropy of God (3:4)—his

unfailing goodness and loving kindness. This sense of beneficence stands out to the recipients of that goodness in stark
contrast to the inhumanity of man in verse 3, highlighting the
darkness of their past with the light of their present experience. Second, Titus was to stress the regenerating and renew-
ing power of the Holy Spirit (3:5). Third, he was to proclaim
the grace of Christ, who makes us heirs with him (3:7). As a
result of this action of the triune God, we have the hope of
eternal life. Fourth, Titus was to stress that the Holy Spirit is
not doled out with a stingy hand, but is "poured out on us generously" (3:6). The young leader was to proclaim these truths
with all certainty and enthusiasm.

Suffering

"Here is a trustworthy saying: 'If we died with him, we will
also live with him; if we endure, we will also reign with him. If
we disown him, he will also disown us; if we are faithless, he
will remain faithful, for he cannot disown himself'" (2 Timothy 2:11-13).

This was one of the hymns of the early church. It emphasiz-
es the fact that the church is heir to the cross of Christ. In the
troubled days we live in, when violence and revolution seem
endemic, our message should prepare people for the most dire
situations. Martin Luther wrote, "If we are put to death out of
loyalty to Christ, we shall also live with him in glory."

Loyalty to Christ will be rewarded, and disloyalty will bring
its own retribution. If we choose to die to earthly ease and
advantage for his sake, there will be heavenly compensations.
Tertullian claimed that the person who is afraid to suffer cannot belong to the One who has greatly suffered. How glad we

should be that there are some things Omnipotence cannot do—"He cannot disown himself."

Self-Discipline

"Train yourself to be godly. For physical training is of some value, but godliness has value for all things, holding promise for both the present life and the life to come. This is a trustworthy saying that deserves full acceptance" (1 Timothy 4:7-9). The picture in these verses is of a gymnasium, where the athletic youth trained for the arena. Here Paul exhorts Timothy not to confine himself merely to pious meditation, but to exercise himself vigorously in godly living. The passage breathes strenuousness and discipline.

The athlete spares no effort nor self-denial to win the prize; he discards everything that impedes progress. This is how the Christian should be. Moral muscle and spiritual sinew come from serious exercise in the realm of the Spirit, and will pay handsome dividends in the life to come.

Physical discipline and exercise is valuable, but when compared with spiritual discipline, its benefits are limited. One results in beauty of physique, the other in life everlasting. One concerns this present time, the other impinges on eternity. Physical training should not be disparaged, however, for the body is the temple of the Holy Spirit (1 Corinthians 3:16-17).

STIR UP THE GIFT

At the ordination of young Timothy, Paul and the elders laid their hands on him, thus passing on the grace-gift of the Spirit, which would equip him as apostolic representative.

Aware of Timothy's weakness, Paul gave him a double exhortation:

"*Do not neglect your gift,* which was given you through a prophetic message when the body of elders laid their hands on you" (1 Timothy 4:14). Don't grow careless of the sacred trust! It was a sovereignly bestowed endowment of the Spirit—not an external operation, but an inward grace. Apparently the efficiency of the gift was not automatic; it could potentially decline. "Don't let it suffer by neglect," was Paul's advice.

"*Fan into flame the gift of God,* which is in you through the laying on of my hands. For God did not give us a spirit of timidity, but a spirit of power, of love and of self-discipline" (2 Timothy 1:6-7). It was not that Timothy required a new endowment. "Stir up that inner fire" is the way J. B. Phillips renders it. The spiritual fire had burned low.

Did Paul sense that Timothy's zeal had begun to wane? A flame doesn't automatically rise higher; it tends to die down. In Timothy's case, there was so much contributing toward the quenching of the flame. "Keep in full flame" or "rekindle" the fire if it has died down! Place fresh fuel on the dying embers!

Paul challenged and stimulated Timothy by directing his attention to the nature of the divine endowment—the *charisma* (gift) of verse 6 goes along with the *pneuma* (spirit) of verse 7. We may well ask certain questions of ourselves: Have we been neglecting the gift? Is the flame burning low in our lives? Does it need stirring up?

14

STRAINING TOWARD THE TAPE

I have fought the good fight, I have finished the race,
I have kept the faith.

2 TIMOTHY 4:7

I n spite of all his achievements and successes, Paul was by
no means self-confident. He had no doubt as to his own
salvation, but he was painfully aware of the possibility of
being disqualified in the race and not reaching the tape. So he
practiced constant self-mastery. "I beat my body and make it
my slave so that after I have preached to others, I myself will
not be disqualified for the prize" (1 Corinthians 9:27).

This apostle of Jesus Christ was no stranger to the inside
of a prison. His visit to Jerusalem (Acts 21:17) around A.D.
58 resulted in a five-year imprisonment—painful and weari-
some for him, but abundantly fruitful for the church. Paul's
imprisonment proved to be anything but lost time, resulting
in the enrichment of the church and the world for the following centuries.

The story of Paul's internment reveals how human malice is

controlled by divine sovereignty. The Jews wanted the prisoner transferred from Caesarea to Jerusalem. Had Festus acceded to their demands, the New Testament may not have had Ephesians, Philippians, Colossians, and Philemon. But God was in ultimate control.

Paul's appeal to Caesar (Acts 25:11) led to two years of imprisonment in Rome, where he enjoyed a measure of liberty. It is to this period we owe 1 and 2 Timothy and Titus. What seem at the time to be tragedies often prove in the long run to be triumphs. It was when John was in a concentration camp that he wrote the Apocalypse. While in Bedford Jail, John Bunyan wrote his immortal *Pilgrim's Progress.*

The manner in which Paul turned even his misfortunes to a positive account should encourage those who are "prisoners" through ill health or other trying circumstances. The story of Paul should hearten and inspire us to be ingenious in seeking ways to use the restricting circumstances of our lives to good account.

Now Paul is about to hand on the torch to young Timothy. "But you, keep your head in all situations," he writes. "Endure hardship, do the work of an evangelist, discharge all the duties of your ministry. For I am already being poured out like a drink offering, and the time has come for my departure. I have fought the good fight, I have finished the race, I have kept the faith. Now there is in store for me the crown of righteousness, which the Lord, the righteous Judge, will award to me on that day" (2 Timothy 4:5-8).

Because he was bringing his own ministry to a close, the elder spiritual statesman urged young Timothy to fulfill his own ministry at whatever cost to himself. The Greek word for "departure" here was often used of loosing the moorings of a boat. The old man was casting off the earthly shoreline, ready to embark for the heavenly shore. Indeed, he could do it with a sense of "mission accomplished." What a model for Timothy—and for us. The torch is now in our hands.

Mission Accomplished

Tradition has it that, as a result of his appeal to Nero, after two trials in A.D. 68, Paul was put to death.

The emperor, it is reported, went on a trip while Paul was in Rome. But during that vacation, one of his favorite mistresses was won to the Lord by Paul. When Nero arrived back home, she was gone, having joined a group of Christians. Nero was so infuriated that he wreaked his vengeance on Paul. They took him out the Ostian way and executed him.

> Yea, through life, death, thro' sorrow and thro' winning,
> He shall suffice me, for He hath sufficed:
> Christ is the end, for Christ is the beginning,
> Christ the beginning, for the end is Christ.
> —*F. W. H. Myers*

NOTE TO THE READER

The publisher invites you to share your response to the message of this book by writing Discovery House Publishers, P.O. Box 3566, Grand Rapids, MI 49501, USA. For information about other Discovery House books, music, videos, or DVDs, contact us at the same address or call 1-800-653-8333. Find us on the Internet at http://www.dhp.org/ or send e-mail to books@dhp.org.